UNDERCURRENTS

Refugees and Asylum-Seekers
in Ireland

UNDERCURRENTS

Other titles in the series

UNDERCURRENTS   Series Editor Carol Coulter

Refugees and Asylum-Seekers in Ireland

PAUL CULLEN

CORK UNIVERSITY PRESS

First published in 2000 by
Cork University Press
University College
Cork
Ireland

British Library Cataloguing in Publication Data
A CIP catalogue record for this book is available from
the British Library

ISBN 1 85918 2429

Typeset by Tower Books, Ballincollig, Co. Cork
Printed by ColourBooks Ltd., Baldoyle, Co. Dublin

Contents

Acknowledgements

Allow me to thank my colleague in *The Irish Times*, Carol Coulter, for the encouragement to write this pamphlet for the Undercurrents series. I am grateful to the staff of Cork University Press for steering me through the niceties of preparing this work for publication. Thanks also to Deirdre for reading earlier drafts and the staff of *The Irish Times* library for their assistance in researching the issue.

Paul Cullen,
April, 2000

Introduction

The arrival of about 10,000 asylum-seekers into Ireland over the past five years has had a massive impact on Irish life, far out of proportion to the numbers involved. The sudden reversal of decades of emigration, and its replacement by immigration from all parts of the globe, has profoundly altered Irish self-identity. It has shattered long - and dearly held beliefs regarding our standards of hospitality and human rights, and it has unleashed dark forces that many – though not all – believed Irish people were immune from. All this has come in the middle of the greatest economic boom the state has experienced, one which has led to massive changes in a previously stagnant employment market. Having exported people for centuries, the Irish economy has suddenly developed a voracious thirst for labour. Ireland is currently enjoying an unprecedented era of prosperity, and can finally look at its European neighbours on terms somewhat approximating to equality. But with our new-found wealth come responsibilities towards those experiencing persecution and those less fortunate than ourselves. There is ample evidence that this message has yet to be grasped by a population more used to taking than giving. The debate over asylum-seekers has come from nowhere to occupy a central position in social and political discourse over the past few years. It has brought the best out of some people and the very worst out of others – bureaucrats, politicians and ordinary people. After the initial surprise, when the numbers started rising, the official reaction was to blame, stigmatise and then criminalise the new arrivals. The processing of applications turned into a bureaucratic shambles and the waste of human potential was enormous.

Several years on, some lessons have been learned. Procedures have improved, more resources have been provided to handle asylum claims and cases are being handled more quickly. But the continuing defects of government policy are obvious; the overweening emphasis on policing aspects; the failure to adopt, and stick to, minimum humanitarian principles; the absence of leadership in anti-racism; the finger-pointing and blaming of a vulnerable category of people; and, most of all, the refusal to separate the issues of asylum and immigration and to develop a cogent policy in the latter area.

In unison with (and in some cases in advance of) our European neighbours, Ireland has progressively pulled down the shutters on asylum-seekers. 'The boat is full' now in Dublin, as it is in the other EU capitals. However, years of clamping down with ever more draconian measures have failed to stem migration from the developing world to the wealthy West. In an unequal and shrinking world, this flow of people is set to continue increasing. Ireland, I argue, will not remain immune from this trend. The rise in asylum-seekers is just one symptom of the rapid and massive change our society is undergoing, and its increasing 'connectedness' with the global economy.

In this pamphlet I examine the experience of the government, the main organs of society and the general population over the past five years in dealing with asylum-seekers and other immigrants. It's a story of failure and missed opportunities, leavened only by a few positive outcomes and hopeful signs for the future. Some lessons have been learned, but even today the widespread ignorance of the issue continues to astonish. This study looks at possible options for the future. It examines the dangers of continuing with the present unbalanced and unfair asylum policies. Any system that excludes the vast majority of asylum-seekers but fails to allow for regulated immigration is doomed to failure. Of late, the government has finally taken some steps in this direction, but this move has been driven by economic rather than humanitarian considerations.

There was no foresight and no advance planning before the asylum-seekers started arriving, and little enough understanding or historical and geographical perspective once they were here. Most worrying now, however, is the continuing lack of any moral or political leadership at the head of Irish society on the issue.

The comment by Eilis Ward about the state's first experience of handling of refugees in 1956 holds true for today: 'It is difficult to escape the conclusion that the Government was primarily, if not exclusively, concerned with its prestige abroad – how it presented itself as a new member of the UN – rather than with the welfare of the Hungarians whom it sought to assist.'[1]

What our political leaders have failed to grasp is that society has changed irrevocably; asylum-seekers and a wide variety of other immigrants are here to stay, and they bring with them a new society that will inevitably become multi-ethnic within a short number of years. This may prove a painful transition for many, especially as so many other changes are already underway in Irish society. But it is, I argue, a certainty to be seized rather than an option to be shunned.

There is also a very practical reason for demanding that the government pay more attention to the asylum issue than it has up to now. Official neglect of asylum-seekers over the past decade has wasted years of people's lives, but it has also cost the state tens of millions of pounds. Today we have thousands of asylum-seekers who are prevented from working and who live on social-welfare entitlements which cost the exchequer £35 million in 1999. At the same time, there are huge labour shortages in the economy, and other migrant workers, from within the EU, are being used to plug the gaps. It is clear that if the state had moved faster to provide the resources to hear asylum cases, the present backlog would not exist. People would either have been deported, if their cases were turned down, or they would have entered the labour force. In neither scenario would they be a burden on the state.

This book is structured as follows. Chapter 1 provides a historical perspective, which is necessary to understand the context in which migration to Ireland is taking place. Developments in Europe and elsewhere are explored in chapter 2, which demonstrates that the numbers of asylum-seekers coming to Ireland is minuscule compared to the overall number of refugees worldwide. Chapter 3 looks at the astonishing development of the asylum issue in Irish society in the 1990s, while chapter 4 provides a critique of the mostly inadequate response of the main organs of that society – the politicians, the Department of Justice, the media and the judiciary – to the phenomenon. Ultimately, this is an issue about people – not regulations or numbers – which is why chapter 5 looks at the issue from the perspective of the asylum-seekers most affected by their move to Ireland. Chapter 6 examines the options for the future and makes a number of recommendations. A glossary is provided to explain the main terms used in the book.

1. Historical perspectives

Irish people tend to think of themselves as an homogenous race, but this is far from the reality. This state has experienced waves of immigration from different sources since the beginning of time. Even a short list of arrivals over the past few thousand years would have to include the Celts, Vikings, Normans, English, Scottish, Spanish, Huguenots and Jews. In the twentieth century, small communities of Hungarians, Chileans, Vietnamese, Cubans, Baha'is and Bosnians have come here.

Many of these people were fleeing war and persecution in their own countries. Traditionally, our treatment of them has been poor; in this century we have done the minimum necessary to keep face internationally in our dealings with refugees, and sometimes (for instance, in the case of Jews who sought to come here to escape Nazi Germany) far less. The government, for reasons of diplomacy, has been careful not to allow Ireland to become a 'back-door' to Britain or the US.[2] Travellers, the one ethnically different group that has been in Ireland for hundreds of years, have suffered racism, exclusion and discrimination for centuries. Authority's attempts to come to terms with their different lifestyle were often incompetent and sometimes malevolent. We have seen the same mistakes that were made with travellers repeated with the first wave of convention refugees in the 1990s.

The standards for Ireland's treatment of refugees in the 1990s were set many decades earlier. After World War II, many countries took in Jewish refugees. Ireland had refused to do so in the 1930s, and persisted with this attitude after the war. The Department of Justice declined to take 100 child survivors of the concentration camps, and called Jews 'a potential irritant in the body politic'.[3] Eventually, after much delay and debate in the corridors of power, a small number of Jewish children were allowed in, but under the strictest conditions. The children came here on a temporary basis, until they were moved elsewhere, and they were the economic and social responsibility of the Irish Jewish community.

Though communities such as the Huguenots were classic examples of refugees from an earlier era, Ireland's first experience of programme refugees in modern times dates from 1956, when we accepted 530 Hungarians. In November of that year, the refugees were taken from Dublin to a disused army camp just outside Limerick. Their experiences were primarily negative, culminating in a hunger strike and by 1958 only sixty-one Hungarians remained in Ireland. Most emigrated to Canada as soon as they got the chance.[4]

> It is difficult to escape the conclusion that the Government was primarily, if not exclusively, concerned with its prestige abroad – how it presented itself as a new member of the UN – rather than with the welfare of the Hungarians whom it sought to assist.
>
> Eilis Ward, 1996

Government thinking at the time is revealed in the 1956 report of the Commission on Emigration and other Population Problems, which devoted just four short paragraphs to immigration. While Ireland should be slow to refuse admission to 'desirable immigrants, the present immigration policy, in our opinion, is as liberal as the circumstances permit', the report concluded.[5] Gertel cites this as evidence of the Irish inability to translate self-pity into empathy for the suffering of 'others'.[6]

The next group of programme refugees to arrive in Ireland were 120 Chileans in 1973, who were forced into exile following the overthrow of the Allende regime. They, too, left as soon as circumstances allowed and only a handful remains.

Then came the Vietnamese, the first Asians to be settled. Some 212 Vietnamese 'boat people' came to Ireland in 1979. Although the majority came from poor, peasant backgrounds, many adapted quickly to Ireland and gained employment, often in the fast-food business. At the beginning of 1996, there were 125 family groups comprising over 600 people in the Vietnamese community, of whom 148 were born in Ireland. A 1997 report found high levels of unemployment in the community.

The treatment of programme refugees improved when responsibility for the area passed from the Department of Defence to the Department of Foreign Affairs in 1985, and a dedicated Refugee Agency was established in 1991. It is intended that the agency will assume responsibility for convention refugees too, but this step has been delayed for years by bickering between government departments.

A group of twenty-six Iranian Baha'is were admitted to the country in 1985, and settled well. In the 1990s, the violent break-up of Yugoslavia resulted in several waves of refugees throughout Europe. The first Bosnians came to Ireland in July 1992 and 770 have been admitted to date. On arrival, they were accommodated in a former nurses' home in Cherry Orchard in Dublin run by the Red Cross. The Refugee Agency now manages this.

In 1999, the Refugee Agency supervised the reception of about 1,000 ethnic Albanian refugees from Kosovo, who were accommodated in hostels and former convents and army homes in a variety of locations outside Dublin. The refugees were well received and well treated, so much so that 80 per cent of them were still in Ireland nine months after NATO forces drove the Serbian army out of Kosovo.

Throughout the 1970s and 1980s, the number of refugees arriving in Ireland individually to seek protection under the 1951 Convention remained minuscule. 'Spontaneous' asylum requests never numbered more than about fifty in the years before 1993. However, this figure was artificially depressed by the strong-arm tactics of the immigration authorities of the day. Many a dazed Cuban or Russian who wandered onto the tarmac at Shannon was hustled back onto a waiting aeroplane before he or she could properly apply for asylum.

The Famine and Irish emigration

No consideration of migration to Ireland would be complete if it failed to take account of the phenomenon of emigration and its effect on Irish policy and psyche. While we have been slow to take in people, we were always very quick to export them.

Emigration scarred our history, but it also fortified our sense of grievance and victimhood, allowing us to forget that many other peoples have suffered the yoke of colonial oppression and have had terrible experiences in their own histories. Gertel refers to Irish attitudes 'encompassing a selfish world-view of morality and self-preservation, often tending toward self-pity'.[7]

The Irish self-view as the underdog, combined with our history of repeated rebellions, made it easy for us to sympathise and side with the Third World in its twentieth-century struggle for freedom and equality. But growing economic success has made this empathy seem hollow in recent years, as Ireland repeatedly sides with the interests of its major (Western) trading partners in political conflicts and trade disputes.

There, then, is little in Ireland's treatment of previous generations of refugees to give cause for comfort. Sentimental expressions of concern aside, the practical experience of outsiders in a closely-knit Irish society has been uncomfortable. Few migrants stayed for long periods and those that did frequently had to contend with a heightened perception that they were 'different' from or 'other' than the rest of the population.

2. A drop in the ocean – European and global perspectives

There is nothing new about people seeking asylum from persecution; there is everything new about them doing it in Ireland. To understand what has happened in Ireland in recent years, you first have to look at developments further afield, both in the European Union and beyond. The policies introduced by the Department of Justice and other government departments are the direct result of developments in the EU; future changes will also be dictated by external circumstances.

Throughout this century, war and other conflicts have sent millions of people fleeing for protection from their homelands. A million people fled the Bolshevik armies in European Russia in 1919–20. Over 320,000 Armenians scattered through Europe a few years later. At the same time, Greece and Turkey expelled their respective minorities, numbering almost two million people. In the 1930s, hundreds of thousands were uprooted during the Spanish Civil War and 250,000 left Germany after Hitler came to power. By 1942, at the height of World War II, there were more than 21 million homeless and displaced people throughout Europe.[8]

After the War, as the Cold War between the US and the USSR intensified, the status of asylum become ideological. The Soviet Bloc kept its dissidents under strict control, but a steady stream of refugees still made it to the West, where they were generally welcomed. Many were highly educated dissidents and, anyway, the numbers involved were quite small. This era lasted until 1989, when the Berlin Wall was torn down and the Soviet Bloc disintegrated. Waves of tumult and change spread throughout Eastern Europe, once more setting people in motion. The post-War German economic miracle came to an end, just as Europe was becoming more attractive to migrants from poor countries in Eastern Europe and the Third World.

The international community took the first steps towards providing formal protection for refugees shortly after World

War II. The 1948 Universal Declaration of Human Rights assured people the right to seek and enjoy asylum. The 1951 Convention relating to the Status of Refugees codified the principle that no one should be returned to a country where their life or freedom would be at risk. It defines a refugee as a person with 'a well-founded fear of being persecuted for reasons of race, religion, nationality, membership of a particular social group or political opinion' and who is outside the country of his nationality.

Until the early 1980s the number of asylum-seekers arriving in Western Europe remained fairly stable at fewer than 100,000 annually. Around 70 per cent came from Eastern Europe and they were rapidly integrated. These were 'well-heeled' refugees who were easily assimilated into Western society; besides, their value as visible proof of the failure of Communism was immense. In emergencies, such as the Hungarian crisis of 1956, the US, Canada, Australia, etc., all willingly offered permanent settlement to refugees – an early form of 'burden-sharing'. Ireland accepted 530 Hungarians, a relatively small number compared to the thousands taken in other Western states. As refugees from the invasion of Hungary by Soviet forces, the new arrivals were particularly popular with anti-Communist elements within the Irish Catholic church.

By the mid-1980s, however, the picture began to change. The instability of the post-Cold War world sent millions into flight. Western Europe spluttered economically and immigration quotas were slashed. Because prospects for regular migration to Western Europe were virtually nil, many would-be migrants now sought entry through the asylum process.

In response to demand, organised trafficking of migrants increased. Smuggling networks spread through Europe, and agents demanded high fees for providing passage to the West. Trafficking is undoubtedly an unsavoury business, particularly when the emphasis is on money, but it should be remembered that this is precisely what heroes such as Raoul Wallenberg and Oskar Schindler engaged in to save Jewish lives during the Nazi era. Nor does it mean that those being trafficked are unworthy of asylum status.

In 1986 the total number of applicants to European States almost doubled to nearly 200,000 and it reached 316,900 in 1989. More applicants came from Africa, Asia and the Middle East. By the time the number of asylum-seekers in Europe reached an unprecedented peak of 696,500 in 1992, governments were applying a sweeping 'zero immigration' policy. (Incredibly, there were just thirty-nine applications for asylum in Ireland in this year.) The emphasis had shifted decisively from one of protecting refugees to exclusion and control.

In the 1990s, Germany took in 350,000 Bosnians and 100,000 Croats. Most have returned home since. In 1999, Kosovans became the latest casualties of the disintegration of Yugoslavia to take flight in large numbers. By 1998, the number of asylum-seekers in Europe had dropped to 332,800, or less than half the 1992 peak. Roughly 45 per cent went to Germany. About 40 per cent of applicants were Europeans, mainly Kosovo Albanians and Turkish Kurds, reflecting two of Europe's most intractable problems.

Clamping down

Western countries responded to the increase in numbers seeking asylum in the early 1990s in a variety of ways. Yet everything they did in this period had but one aim: to limit access as much as possible. For the first time, the EU took major steps towards co-ordinating the asylum policies of its member states. Central to this reform is the concept of the 'first country application', whereby a person is allowed apply for asylum in just one EU state. If the person travels on to another EU state, in most cases he will be returned to the first state to have his application considered there. The measure is designed to stop asylum-seekers from 'shopping around', but it has led to concerns about 'chain expulsions', where a person who has been deported is passed through a series of countries with ever lower human rights standards. In some cases, the last link in the chain is the asylum-seeker's home country, although it was never the professed intention of the EU state that first deported the person that he should end up in the very place he fled. For example, an Algerian asylum-seeker could in theory be deported from Ireland to Belgium to Germany and thence to Algeria, even though the Irish government does not deport applicants directly to Algeria. Since the process is shrouded in secrecy, it is highly unlikely that anyone in Ireland would subsequently learned anything about the fate of such an asylum-seeker in his homeland.

Harmonisation of policies has also entailed a reduction of welfare benefits. For instance, most parts of Germany now give assistance in kind rather than in cash and at 80 per cent of the level a needy citizen receives. In 1998, it further reduced benefits to asylum-seekers entering the country illegally or whose applications had been rejected. In October 1997, the Netherlands introduced a system in which new arrivals are housed in tents and put on a 'waiting list' for proper accommodation.

Another deterrent is the threat of detention. At any one time, one in ten asylum-seekers is detained in Austria. Some are jailed with ordinary criminals. Those arriving at Frankfurt airport are held in a closed facility until their claim has been decided. The government refuses to call it detention because it argues that they are free to leave at any time – back to the country they came from. In Northern Ireland, the authorities have begun to detain asylum-seekers, even though the numbers involved are very small. At the time of writing, the British government has announced that it intends to set up its first privately run internment camp for asylum-seekers. In the US, undocumented asylum-seekers are generally detained until final resolution of their case, a process which can take months or even years. According to Amnesty International, many are detained with criminal prisoners, often in harsh conditions; many are subjected to frequent strip searches, and are shackled or handcuffed when taken to hearings outside the detention facility.

As the UNHCR (United Nations High Commissioner for Refugees) State of the World report for 1998 notes, there is a growing tendency for governments to interpret the criteria for refugee status in an increasingly restrictive manner. The attempt by European states to implement a narrow form of who can qualify as a bona fide refugee is arguably the most serious erosion of asylum standards. Western states have dedicated themselves to restricting access to asylum without infringing humanitarian principles. But this trick can only be achieved by bending the definition of asylum.

In recent years, governments have developed the idea of excluding people who have been persecuted by so-called 'non-state agents' like rebels or religious extremists. Germany's Federal Administrative Court, for example, ruled that persons who fled Afghanistan's Taliban could not qualify for refugee status because the Taliban do not represent a recognised government. Similar judgments have seen the rejection of asylum applications by Bosnian Muslims, Somalis and Algerians. In contrast, Sweden, the UK and the Netherlands have taken a more liberal view.

But even the 1951 definition of a refugee is noteworthy as much for what it omits as for what it includes. Drawn up with the massive post-war migration in Europe in mind, it hardly meets modern needs. We talk about refugees from famine, floods, plague and war, but most of these people are not strictly refugees according to the definition. To prove yourself a refugee you must first of all establish that you are being 'persecuted'. The definition is pre-occupied with state persecution, and makes little allowance for 'non-state agents' of persecution, for example, the Russian mafia or religious extremists active in a number of countries.

The vexed issue of 'economic refugees' is not addressed. Most of the millions who left Ireland over the past 150 years fell into this category. The UN distinguishes between 'economic migrants' and refugees, but it accepts that the distinction is sometimes blurred. For example, famine has become a weapon of war in many conflicts, but are those fleeing hunger also fleeing persecution?

So Europe has been 'raising the bar' in response to the increased flow of refugees. As a result, in 1997 only 11 per cent of European applicants were recognised as refugees under the 1951 Convention.

How the EU has moved to stem the flow of refugees

From the start of the 1990s, the EU has progressively tightened its controls on the flow of refugees. While member states agreed on the economic benefits of freedom of movement, it was determined that this would only apply between EU members. In June 1990, they signed the Schengen Implementation Agreement, which envisaged the end of border controls and free travel between member states. Schengen marked a key milestone on the road to Fortress Europe.

In the same month, states also signed the Dublin Convention, the first major step by Europe to co-ordinate national asylum policies. Its main aim is to establish the country responsible for examining individual asylum requests. Asylum-seekers would be deterred from 'shopping around'. The convention came into force in 1997.

The Maastricht Treaty in 1992 empowered EU Justice and Home Affairs ministers to establish a framework for a Europe-wide asylum policy. Ten months later, they approved the first three non-binding Resolutions and Conclusions:

1   the safe third country concept, allowing states to refuse individuals access to their asylum procedures if the applicant could have sought protection in another 'safe' country
2   the creation of the category of 'manifestly unfounded' asylum applications, giving states wide scope for rejecting asylum requests on formal grounds and for limiting appeal possibilities
3   the creation of 'safe countries of origin', for which accelerated procedures apply in the case of claimants coming from countries in which there is generally deemed to be no serious risk of persecution

Two years later, the first re-admission agreements were signed between EU and non-EU states. Today, a dense web of such accords is in place, mostly with states in Eastern Europe and North Africa. In June 1995 the Resolution on Minimum Guarantees for Asylum Procedures put in place a number of important safeguards for asylum-seekers. This prevented their removal from a country during an appeal, stipulated that a specialised authority should examine asylum claims, and held that applicants should be informed about the procedure and their rights and duties in a language they understood. The following year, however, a non-binding Joint Position allowed states to adopt a restrictive interpretation of the refugee definition, so as, for example, to rule out 'non-state' persecution. The 1997 Amsterdam Treaty foresaw binding measures leading to the harmonisation of social assistance for asylum-seekers, temporary protection of refugees in the event of any mass influx and burden-sharing among member-states.

The measures have largely achieved their desired effect; from 1987 to 1998, the acceptance rate for asylum applications in the EU fell from 50 per cent to 10 per cent. This is not a universal trend; in Canada, for example, 70 per cent of applications were accepted in 1994–5. Rather than tinker with existing rules, the Austrian presidency of the EU in 1998 sought to dismantle the 1951 Convention relating to the Status of Refugees. According to a confidential strategy paper prepared by the Austrians, the Refugee Convention was an outdated instrument and should be replaced by a 'new approach' to refugee protection. This new approach should be 'more politically oriented', where protection would not be seen as a 'subjective individual right, but rather a political offer on the part of the host country'. The Austrian paper was submitted in confidence to the K4 Committee of the EU in July 1998. (K4 is a secretive high-level committee of civil servants from the member states, including Ireland, which discusses policy matters relating to immigration and asylum.) The paper was leaked and caused a storm in the media and the European parliament. The Austrian government was forced to withdraw the paper and submitted a watered-down version to the K4 committee later in the year. However, recent political developments in Austria make it likely that these proposals may be resurrected in the near future.[9]

Many Western countries have imposed sanctions on airline and ferry carriers that transport illegal immigrants, and Ireland is following suit. In the UK, for example, there is a fine of £2,000 per passenger on any transport operator bringing in passengers who lack valid travel documents or a valid visa where one is required. The law is strictly applied. Since the Act came into force in March 1987, fines totalling over £89 million have been imposed on airlines and shipping companies. Further restrictions are in the pipeline in many countries. In the UK, for example, the 1998 White Paper on asylum-seekers recommends a new support system for asylum-seekers, separate from the main system. The Irish government, which is closely watching developments in Britain, has signalled its intention to move to a voucher-support system around the time this happens in the UK in April 2000.

Up to now, the Dublin Convention has applied to only a small number of asylum cases. Inter-state co-operation has fallen short of the levels hoped for by the architects of the convention and many migrants have frustrated the regulations by arriving in an EU state without any documentation. In such cases, the convention cannot be applied. In response, EU governments have formulated new measures to further tighten up procedures. Finger-printing of all asylum-seekers is the most controversial proposal, but accelerated procedures are also being considered in cases where applicants have no documentation.

Western governments are entitled to take whatever measures they see fit to regulate immigration across their borders. However, the question arises as to whether human rights provisions are being infringed in the move towards greater restrictions. In 1998, when several EU states started deporting Kosovan refugees, the European Parliament was moved to ask governments to stop this practice. Subsequent events showed that the parliament was right.

'The challenge', says Stefan Teloken of the European Council for Refugees in Europe (ECRE), 'is to find a reasonable balance between the states' legitimate interests and those of refugees'.[10] The ECRE believes a more equitable 'sharing' of refugees among member states could help avoid further restrictive asylum measures. But the individual states are still arguing among themselves about their level of responsibility. In any case, the behaviour of immigration officials on the ground seldom accords with the lofty pronouncements of central government.

Finally, this consideration of asylum issues in Europe requires a global perspective. Estimates of the number of refugees worldwide vary, depending on whether people who are internally displaced in their own country are included. However, one estimate is that their number has grown from eight to fifteen million over the past decade. Yet only 5 per cent of refugees try to seek sanctuary in Europe; poor countries with a fraction of the wealth of EU states put up the rest. Ireland's share of this burden – about 10,000 asylum-seekers in a decade – is clearly derisory.

3. The asylum-seeker phenomenon

As noted in the last chapter, just thirty-nine people applied for asylum in Ireland in 1992, the year in which the total number of applications in the rest of Western Europe was peaking at almost 700,000. It was inevitable from that year that the wave of immigration breaking over Europe would hit Ireland; the only curiosity is that it caught so many people by surprise.

In the years that followed, the number of asylum applications handled by the Department of Justice increased almost exponentially. It reached 424 in 1995, 3,883 in 1997 and 4,626 in 1998. The asylum-seeker issue became a topic of everyday comment and political debate, yet for some time the department continued to process applications at a snail's pace. The number of staff dealing with applications remained small until the section was expanded in 1998.

In the first six months of 1999, a further 1,975 applications were received and the total backlog stood at over 6,000. Since this figure includes anomalies such as double or lapsed applications, a better guide to the total number of asylum-seekers in Ireland is derived from the number claiming social-welfare benefits. In October 1999, the Department of Social, Community and Family Affairs reported that it had a total of 9,062 asylum-seekers on its books.

Asylum-seekers are a disparate bunch; since 1991, more than 100 different nationalities have sought refuge in Ireland. In 1998, disproportionate numbers came from Nigeria (40 per cent) and Romania (22 per cent), according to figures provided by the department. Algeria, Libya, Angola and Congo (15 per cent together), were the other main countries of origin.[11] The figures for 1999 were similar. In that year, Romania topped the list, with 1,678 applications. Next came Nigeria, with 1,155 applications. There were 459 applications from Poland, 219 from Kenya, 206 from Algeria, 197 from Moldova and 175 from Congo/Zaire. The remainder of the top ten countries comprised Slovakia (141 applications), Angola (125) and Russia (113).

Two-thirds of asylum applicants were living in private rented accommodation in 1998, and one-third in hostels and B&Bs, according to the Department of Social, Community and Family Affairs.[12] Asylum-seekers vary greatly in age, although most tend to be in their twenties and thirties. In January 2000, the Irish Refugee Council reported that seventy-four children, separated from their parents or carers, were seeking refugee status. The youngest child was thirteen but most were around fifteen or sixteen.

Why Ireland?

Many reasons have been put forward for Ireland's increasing popularity with asylum-seekers. Usually, these are advanced together with a sense of surprise, as though this country, which is one of the twenty richest democracies in the world, could not *possibly* prove attractive to people from other, poorer countries. Nothing could be further from the truth. Primarily, though, the phenomenon is part of a worldwide trend; today, there are more refugees in the world than ever. Some estimates put the total number as high as 50 million (this estimate includes people internally displaced in their own countries). Yet in many other Western countries the shutters are coming down, and curbs on immigration have been introduced throughout the EU. At the same time, Ireland's international profile is higher than before, and the success of the 'Celtic Tiger' has not gone unnoticed. News travels fast and far these days, thanks to the Internet, and people travel fast too.

As the Department of Justice frequently points out, Britain's social-welfare regime is less generous towards refugees than it used to be. Even Germany, for so long the main destination for asylum-seekers coming to the EU, is significantly less generous than Ireland. The standard payment per person is £180 a month, compared to £288 in Ireland. Most asylum-seekers in Germany are given vouchers or coupons rather than cash and the cost of their accommodation and heating is first deducted. Only a basic £33 a month is guaranteed to be paid in cash as 'pocket money'. Unlike Ireland, their freedom of movement is highly circumscribed and they can be fined for travelling outside the district to which they have been assigned. In addition, levels of racism are higher, arguably, in Germany and most other EU states than they are in Ireland.

All of this makes Ireland – easily reached in the same common travel area as Britain – more attractive for some asylum-seekers. Finally, once a few refugees come to a country and become established, it is inevitable that more from the same region or country will follow.

Asylum versus immigration

The Department of Justice maintains that Ireland is not an immigrant nation, but this claim does not hold up to scrutiny. Between 1992 and 1997, 220,000 people immigrated into Ireland (while 197,000 emigrated). In 1997 alone, immigration hit 44,000, and there was a net inflow of population of 15,000. Of this 44,000, 20,000 came from the UK, 8,100 from other EU states, 6,600 from the US and 9,300 from the rest of the world. Many, if not most, were returning Irish emigrants.

Ireland does not limit the number of Irish people returning home, British people who wish to work in this state, or EU nationals who come here. In addition, about 4,500 new applicants from outside the EU are given work permits every year. But since most of these are reserved for people with specialist skills, for many would-be immigrants the asylum option represents their best chance of getting into Ireland, at least on a temporary basis.

The picture is one of considerable movement in and out of Ireland. The difference, of course, is that up to recent years, immigrants were largely Irish and virtually all white. But even in 1997, refugee numbers accounted for no more than about 9 per cent of total immigration. The EU is host to about 8 million non-EU nationals, or 2.3 per cent of its total population. In Ireland the total non-national population is lower, at 50,000, or 1.4 per cent of the population, but even this figure is inflated as it includes EU nationals other than British.

The vast majority of asylum-seekers occupy a 'grey' area between those who have been granted asylum and those who have been deported after their applications were turned down. Even after the long years of waiting, the 'limbo' situation persists after an application has been refused, as asylum-seekers wait to see if they may yet remain in the state. Leave to remain in the state is granted at the discretion of the Minister for Justice. It may be accorded to a person who does not fully meet the requirements of the definition of the 1951 Convention, but who the minister decides should be allowed to remain in the state on humanitarian grounds. The growing numbers of people granted leave to stay on these grounds constitute a category of 'second-class citizens'. 'They will be relegated to a secondary legal and social status within Irish society, whereby ministerial discretion, rather than the law, will determine most of their entitlements.'[13] Family reunification, entitlement-to-travel documents and right to work are all at the minister's discretion.

This category of asylum-seeker is likely to grow in the coming years. Many applicants have put down roots in Ireland in the years they spent waiting for their cases to be processed. In other cases, the state is unable to find a way of returning a refused applicant to their home country. Somalia, for example, has no functioning government and is clearly not a safe place to return an asylum-seeker to whose application has been turned down.

When Irish people have difficulties with officialdom, they often ask friends, family or political representatives to intervene on their behalf. However, asylum-seekers, newly arrived in a country and often unable to speak the language, lack access to these kinds of networks. Ministerial discretion is all very well if you're from a politician's home town, but it's a different matter for a black asylum-seeker with no influence or access to lawyers or politicians. For this reason, any future review of asylum law needs to look closely at the uncertain status of people granted humanitarian leave to stay in Ireland.

Employment and study rights

After considerable debate, the government decided in 1999 to give some asylum-seekers the right to work. The measure was crudely designed to apply only to applicants who had been waiting for more than twelve months and who arrived in Ireland before the cut-off date in July 1999. This move, no more than a recognition of the practical reality of the Celtic Tiger economy and its voracious need for cheap labour, is less generous than regulations in force in neighbouring EU states. Germany, Sweden and the UK, for example, generally allow the right to work after three months, four months and six months respectively if a case is pending. Finland grants this right after three months under certain conditions. An asylum-seeker in Spain may apply for a provisional work permit. Belgium allows the right to work after the application is considered admissible. Asylum-seekers are not allowed to work in Denmark, France, Italy and the Netherlands. But all these countries process applications relatively rapidly, in about one year.[14] The exception is Italy, where an application and appeal can take anywhere between five and eight years.

The department says that giving asylum-seekers early access to employment 'is treating them as economic migrants, will act as a "pull factor" and will encourage further abuses of the asylum system . . .'.[15] In seeming confirmation of this view, there was a sharp upswing in the number of asylum-seekers coming to Ireland in the months after the limited right to work was announced. However, this could also be attributed to seasonal factors, which lead to greater migration across Europe in the warm summer months.

The extended debate about the right to work grew increasingly absurd in 1998 and 1999 as it became apparent that asylum-seekers and other immigrants were being employed – illegally – in great numbers in the Celtic Tiger economy. The evidence for this is to be found in almost any restaurant or hotel kitchen in Dublin and beyond, where immigrant labour has been used to make up for the shortage of local workers. Although some media and politicians have claimed that asylum-seekers are drawn here by welfare benefits, common sense tells us that the abundance of work is the crucial factor. Asylum-seekers work in low-skill areas because jobs are plentiful and language is generally not a barrier. However, many asylum-seekers arrive in Ireland with high levels of education acquired in their own countries; in a limited survey completed between October 1997 and March 1998, Fr Michael Begley found that only 2 per cent of asylum-seekers were unskilled.[16]

The state has been phlegmatic in its response to the education needs of asylum-seekers and their children. Until 1999, no special resources were available in schools to assist the children of non-English-speaking parents. Finally, the Department of Education then sanctioned the appointment of fourteen support teachers to the primary schools in Dublin and Ennis, where most of the 1,600 non-English speaking pupils were located. This year, additional supports have been announced for schools with concentrations of pupils whose first language in not English. Meanwhile, the teaching of English to adult asylum-seekers is mostly in the hands of voluntary groups, such as the scheme run by the African Cultural Network and staff and students at Dublin City University.

It is clear that the official attitude views the period spent waiting for a decision as being equivalent to being in purgatory. The asylum-seeker is obliged to suffer for this time. Access to support for education and training courses is blocked. Even to attend Post-Leaving Certificate courses, which are free and grant-aided for the rest of the population, an asylum-seeker is required to fork out the overseas tuition fee of up to £2,000 a year.

Social welfare

In spite of the public perception that asylum-seekers receive special treatment, they in fact receive the lowest level of support available under the social-welfare system. All asylum-seekers are entitled to the current individual weekly payment for social welfare assistance (SWA) of about £72 a week, which is the lowest in the system. They are not permitted to work, except under the limited scheme announced in summer 1999, and they may not 'sign on'. Couples receive £115.20 and people with children receive an additional £13.20 per child per week.

In October 1999, some 5,377 SWA payments were being made in respect of 9,062 asylum-seekers – the larger figure includes dependants and about 2,000 children. This is an increase of 50 per cent since the beginning of 1998. About 90 per cent of payments are in the Eastern Health Board area, especially in Dublin's inner city and West Dublin. Payments to asylum-seekers accounted for about 12 per cent of total SWA spending in 1998. One out of every five SWA recipients is an asylum-seeker. The cost of social-welfare payments in 1998 was about £22 million, according to the Department of Social, Community and Family

Affairs, about half of one per cent of its total budget. By the end of 1999, the annual cost is expected to have risen to £35 million, the department estimated in October of that year. This includes the money paid to private landlords and hostel owners who provide accommodation for asylum-seekers.

Benefits vary greatly within the EU. As I have shown, in most parts of Germany, for example, all support comes in the form of benefits in kind, with a small cash payment for everyday needs. Britain is close to moving towards a similar system, and the current Minister for Justice, Mr O'Donoghue, has also signalled his interest in this 'voucher' system for Ireland.

In Ireland, refugees are generally free to live where they choose, and rely on the local health board for assistance in finding accommodation. Most stay in hostels for short periods before finding private rented accommodation of their own. The Netherlands, Belgium and Denmark, in contrast, provide reception centres or similar communal accommodation.

It is clear from the above that asylum-seekers constitute only a small proportion of immigration into Ireland. The extraordinary amount of attention focused on this minority can only be explained by the fact that many asylum-seekers are not white. In spite of repeated assertions to the contrary, asylum-seekers do not receive special or generous treatment from the social-welfare system, although the minimum payments they receive are large in comparison to income levels in developing countries. The extraordinary rise in applications in recent years is the result of two main 'push' and 'pull' factors: the growth in migration worldwide, which should have been foreseen; and the improvement in Ireland's economic fortunes, which has exceeded all expectations.

4. Response of official Ireland

An examination of the reception and determination procedures for those seeking asylum in Ireland throughout the current decade is revealing. It portrays indisputable inadequacies in our administrative responses, a reluctant building of institutional structures for refugee protection and assistance, and lethargy in adapting to radically changing realities.[17]

When the figures began to dramatically change, the state was ill prepared, ill equipped to deal with and institutionally ignorant of the complex needs of asylum-seekers.[18]

Ireland's response to the arrival of large numbers of asylum-seekers in the 1990s has been shameful. The Department of Justice, politicians and the media have at various times abused a vulnerable group of people for selfish gain or to cover up inaction or incompetence on their own part. Only the courts and to some extent the Eastern Health Board emerge from this episode with much credit. The hope now can only be that the mistakes of the 1990s have been learned and will not be repeated.

Politicians largely washed their hands of the issue, and therefore deserve much of the blame for the state's tardy response to the increase in asylum-seekers coming to Ireland. Successive ministers for justice left the determination and execution of policy to their department officials, even when it was becoming obvious that important issues of human rights and pluralism had arisen. Populist backbenchers adopted a two-faced approach, especially before elections, which saw them make high moral statements in public while at the same time attacking asylum-seekers when canvassing on voters' doorsteps.

The department has been left to determine the standards that should apply, and it has done this until recently in a mean-spirited, mistrustful and blinkered way. Officials repeatedly cast doubt on the bona fides of most asylum-seekers without ever adducing any evidence. They ignored the fact that if, as they claim, most applications were bogus, this should mean that the asylum-seekers would be refused and deported. The problem, as it was seen by the department, would simply wither away.

Since the foundation of the State, the Department of Justice has played the lead role in formulating and executing official policy on refugees. Prior to the Refugee Act 1996, Ireland discharged its responsibilities to asylum-seekers and refugees by way of an 'informal agreement' between the department and the Office of the United Nations High Commissioner for Refugees (UNHCR).

Up to 1985, no written agreement existed and it was only in that year that the terms of agreement were outlined in a letter from the Department to the UNHCR. The Fakih High Court case made this binding.[19] The need for legislation in this area was recognised by the Interdepartmental Committee on Non-Irish Nationals in its interim report in 1994, in which it was noted that Ireland 'was almost unique in not having a legislative base for the processing of applications for asylum'. In that year, there were 362 applications for asylum.

The committee also noted that

> there has been disquiet expressed by the public and by organisations concerned with human rights in the operation of the existing procedures for dealing with applications for asylum. Criticisms have been levelled against the Department of Justice, in particular, to the effect that the procedures set out in the 1985 agreement with the UNHCR have not always been as rigorously followed as they might be. It has been argued that access to legal advice and assistance as well as proper interpretation has, at best, been restrictive. Criticism has been levelled also at the lack of any formal right of appeal.[20]

Following this report, a Refugee Bill was introduced to the Dail in 1994 but in light of the numerous amendments made, it was withdrawn and replaced by the Refugee Bill 1995. This was widely seen as a progressive piece of legislation, which addressed issues such as the rights to residence, health care and social welfare as well as access to the courts. It provided for an independent refugee commissioner and a Refugee Appeals

Board. The bill didn't address the right to work, or the provision of translation facilities during interviews with asylum applicants. It listed twelve separate criteria for 'manifestly unfounded' applications, and provided a 'fast-track' mechanism for dealing with these. The present Fianna Fail Minister for Justice, John O'Donoghue, was then in opposition and responded thus to the proposed legislation: 'This is an enlightened Bill and its provisions will be of considerable assistance to the unfortunate asylum-seekers and refugees.' However, numerous amendments were put forward and there was considerable delay before the Bill was passed in 1996, just before the Rainbow Coalition government lost power.

Developments since the Refugee Act 1996

These hold-ups were as nothing compared to the delays in implementing the legislation that followed the change of government. The most straightforward sections of the Act were implemented in August 1997; these covered the definition of a refugee, acceptance of the principle of non-refoulement, and a provision allowing for the ratification of the Dublin Convention. The rest of the Act, including the important sections relating to an independent assessment of asylum claims, has not been implemented, and is widely regarded now as a 'dead duck'. Mr O'Donoghue gave as a reason for not implementing the legislation a High Court challenge by a former minister, Patrick Cooney, over age restrictions for the post of refugee commissioner. However, a year after Mr Cooney lodged his case, the government had yet to challenge his injunction. It clearly suited the new government and its officials not to move on the legislation passed by a more liberal administration.

As the government continued to drag its heels, Mr O'Donoghue introduced a new argument in favour of non-implementation, claiming that the single refugee commissioner provided for in the Act could not handle the level of decisions required. This was true; in the interim, the level of asylum applications had increased ten-fold. However, a simple amending piece of legislation would have got around this difficulty by providing for the appointment of multiple commissioners. The Labour TD, Pat Upton, published such a bill but, not surprisingly, Mr O'Donoghue showed no interest in it.

The failure to implement the Refugee Act left thousands of asylum-seekers in a legal and administrative limbo. There was still no independent body to judge their claims; there isn't to this day. They had no access to legal aid, and many were left to face into the daunting process without any help. At appeal stage, the final decision in their cases rested with the minister, acting on the recommendation of an appeals authority. There was still great uncertainty about 'manifestly unfounded' and Dublin Convention cases. Playing for time in the face of criticism from many quarters, the Department commissioned a comparative study of refugee legislation in EU member states. The results of this have never been published. An inter-departmental committee was set up to examine all aspects of the asylum-seeker issue.

The record of the Department of Justice

The view of the Department of Justice is that Ireland is not a country of immigration, and it will do nothing that might encourage people to come from non-EU states. The mentality underlying its primary responsibility, that of policing and maintaining security in the state, seeps into dealings with asylum-seekers, where officials sometimes give the impression that they are the wardens fending off 'the barbarians at the gate'.

The department strictly observes the Geneva Convention, but its interpretation of international human rights instruments could be said to be narrow and minimalist. It is particularly concerned not to create any 'pull factor' for non-EU immigrants, and slavishly follows developments in Britain to ensure this. Lawyers and other observers say the department behaves 'correctly' in legal terms in investigating applications for asylum. However, a recurring complaint made by asylum applicants to one group of researchers was that department interviewers appeared to be working on the basis of 'guilty until proved innocent' with interviews being conducted in an atmosphere of 'disbelief'.[21]

How else can it be explained why, of 158 appeals against deportation under the Dublin Convention between 1997 and mid-1998, not a single one was allowed? The department has argued that the deportations were based on 'established facts' but as opposition politicians pointed out, these decisions were based on written materials rather than oral hearings. The anomaly has become particularly plain since the appeals authorities started their work – and proceeded to overturn up to one-third of original decisions.

Other writers have adverted to the near-obsessive secrecy of the department. As Faughnan points out, we know virtually nothing about asylum-seekers as a group; where they come from, their age, marital status, number of children, where they're living, their background and how many have applied for Irish citizenship.[22] The department even withheld basic figures on the country of origin of asylum-seekers, and told journalists this information could not be provided. The statistics were revealed only when reporters invoked Freedom of Information legislation.

The Dublin Convention, which provides for most asylum applications to be dealt with in the first EU state in which an asylum-seeker lands, was especially welcomed by department officials. Because Ireland is an island located far from the main transit routes used by migrants, few asylum-seekers can come here without first setting foot in one of our EU neighbours. Theoretically, then, they could be returned to that state to have their applications processed there. In practice, however, co-operation between member states has seen inadequate, and the department has been unable to return as many asylum-seekers as it might have liked. In addition, many of those arriving in Ireland come without any papers or evidence that they may have transited through, say, Britain or France. As a result, officials are forced to deal with their applications here.

Under new direction and with increased funding at its disposal, the department has begun to reform the way it handles asylum applications. The asylum unit was established in 1996 with just three staff, but subsequently the unit has expanded rapidly. Staffing increased to 16 in 1997, 72 in 1998 and about 144 the following year. However, many of these additional staff are retired civil servants and Gardai who have been employed on a temporary basis to help clear the backlog of applications. Privately, refugee groups have questioned the suitability of such staff, whose working career has been spent in a more insular, closed, Ireland, to deal with the new realities of international human rights. The Dublin office of the United Nations High Commissioner for Refugees provided brief training, but some observers have criticised the suitability of the new staff to process asylum claims. In 1998, the department finally opened its long-awaited 'one-stop shop' in Dublin. The centre on Lower Mount Street handles asylum applications, as well as housing the refugee unit of the Eastern Health Board and a medical screening service.

Throughout this period the UNHCR has had a key monitoring and training role. The high commissioner's representative in London is accredited to both the UK and Ireland. After some delay, the UNHCR opened a liaison office in Dublin in April 1998; initially, it operated from a room in the department's headquarters on St Stephen's Green and later moved to the 'one-stop shop' before finding independent premises.

Though the number arriving continued at high levels, some inroads were made into the backlog. By January 1999, there were 6,699 cases on hand, and only 10 of these went back to 1995. By the end of the year, the department's hopes foundered once more as numbers surged to over 1,000 applications a month. At the end of the year, the backlog stood at 8,700. Some 7,762 applications for asylum were received, about double the level two years previously. Applications were particularly high in the second half of the year – in defiance of previous seasonal trends – and December's figure of 1,255 applications was the highest recorded.

However, the department did manage to process 5,248 cases in 1999. Some 4,737 were refused. More than two-thirds of the 511 people granted refugee status had been refused at the first stage, and were successful on appeal. Also in 1999, the High Court ruled that some of the department's powers to deport 'non-nationals' under the 1935 Aliens Act were unconstitutional. Having dithered over the Refugee Act for three years, the Department took just twelve days to introduce to the Dail new legislation designed to restore its powers of deportation.

While the Government aimed to have the new Bill rushed through the Oireachtas in a fortnight, they hadn't reckoned with the determined stance of the Opposition and human rights groups. The Minister, Mr O'Donoghue, eventually agreed to amend the Immigration Bill to include some elements of the discarded legislation of three years earlier. Some seventy-four amendments were taken in one vote in the Dáil in July 1999 as the Government rushed through the measure.[23]

While asylum-seekers were unhappy at the use of immigration legislation to remedy defects in the asylum process, the result was that all asylum procedures were placed on a statutory footing for the first time. However, the fact that both asylum and immigration issues were being dealt with in the same piece of legislation only further compounded the public confusion as to the distinction between the two issues.

In July 1999, following months of public pressure and significant and ill-disguised disagreement between the government parties on the issue, some asylum-seekers were finally given the right to work. However, the measure was highly circumscribed; it applied only to those asylum-seekers who had arrived in Ireland before the day of the announcement, and who had been waiting for a decision for at least twelve months. The onus was placed on employers to obtain work permits for individual asylum-seekers, and prohibitive fees were applied. The requirement that employers pay £25 a month or £125 a year acted as a serious disincentive to employing asylum-seekers. There was no entitlement to switch to FÁS training schemes, or to apply for jobs at National Manpower offices. The result was confusion at first, as it became apparent that none of the relevant government departments had made any plans to implement the decision. Thereafter, the take-up was slow, because of the limitations of the scheme outlined above. Three months after the measure was introduced, only fifteen permits had been issued. What should have been a humanitarian gesture had been transformed, through mean-mindedness and bad planning, into another botched job.

In Autumn 1999, the number of asylum-seekers coming to Ireland increased again, a trend the Department of Justice was not slow to blame – off the record, of course – on the disputed decision to allow asylum-seekers to work.

Other government departments and health boards

Although the Department of Justice is the main department involved in the asylum cases, many other areas of national and local administration also have responsibilities for asylum-seekers. The list includes the Departments of Foreign Affairs, Health & Children, Social, Community and Family Affairs, Environment and Education; the Refugee Agency; the health boards; the local authorities; and the Red Cross. This is the problem: with so many agencies involved, no-one has been prepared to take the lead responsibility or to counter the largely negative and blinkered view of the Department of Justice.

The Eastern Health Board provides a number of services for asylum-seekers, both directly and on an agency basis. As you might expect, the board provides medical services for asylum-seekers and refugees. But in addition to this, it provides an emergency accommodation placement service on behalf of local authorities (primarily Dublin Corporation) from which it recoups the cost. It also pays asylum-seekers supplementary welfare allowance, rent allowance and other social welfare benefits, and recoups the cost from the Department of Social, Community and Family Affairs.

The accommodation service is a clumsy, complicated system, inherited from the time when the EHB was assigned the responsibility of finding accommodation for homeless persons; the newly arrived asylum-seekers were simply lumped in with local homeless people for administrative convenience. The section of the EHB responsible for finding accommodation for asylum-seekers and homeless people has moved at least three times. On each occasion, unruly scenes among the board's customers and disruption and industrial action by staff preceded the move, as each office in turn was overwhelmed by the increasing number of new arrivals. Scenes of utter chaos were common, as ill-trained and ill-equipped staff attempted in cramped offices to meet the needs of asylum-seekers from a huge number of different countries and backgrounds.

As the number of asylum-seekers continued to grow, the Department of Justice secured funding for hundreds of new staff to process applications. Yet little or no additional resources were provided to bolster the EHB offices dealing with asylum-seekers. It was only in late 1999 when huge queues formed outside the department's refugee-applications centre on Mount Street – the current home of the EHB's accommodation service – that staff were finally goaded into taking decisive industrial action. Subsequently, approval was given for the hiring of sixteen additional staff.

As the board itself admits, it is not a housing agency and it does not have the specialist resources to assess whether accommodation for asylum-seekers complies with planning legislation or building regulations. Responsibility for these functions rests with the local authorities. As a result, hundreds of asylum-seekers found themselves cooped up in overcrowded hostels and B&Bs. Rooms were partitioned, vertically and even horizontally, as greedy landlords sought to maximise their revenue. It wasn't unusual to have up to twenty people sharing the same room. There was clear evidence that some landlords were defrauding the EHB by claiming B&B rates for asylum-seekers who were actually being accommodated in rented flats.

It was only in 1998 that the authorities got to grips with this situation, and started enforcing the standard controls. A number of hostels went out of business and others were forced to undertake major renovations to improve the standard of accommodation. However, the attitude towards asylum-seeker accommodation still seems somewhat lax; for example, when the Department of Justice placed newspaper advertisements in October 1999 seeking accommodation outside Dublin, no mention was made of the need for the accommodation to meet planning regulations.

By late 1999, the EHB had 2,800 asylum-seekers in emergency accommodation in Dublin. A further 6,000 were in private rented accommodation. With over 1,000 new arrivals a month, the board was unable to cope. It started turning away asylum-seekers in large numbers, and alerted the Department of Health & Children of the crisis. The EHB also provides a voluntary health screening service for asylum-seekers and refugees. This includes screening for TB, and Hepatitis B and C, as well as immunisation against diphtheria. The issue of a compulsory testing programme has been raised by some city councillors but rejected by the health professionals responsible for assessing the health of asylum-seekers.

Until very recently, Dublin was home to almost 90 per cent of asylum-seekers in Ireland. Apart from Dublin and Ennis, which is close to Shannon airport, there are no other concentrations of asylum-seekers or refugees in the state. This is no accident. While it is true that many immigrants are drawn to big cities, it is equally true that many local authorities and health boards have done as little as possible to accommodate or make welcome convention refugees.

This applies not just to rural Ireland, but also to major cities such as Cork and Galway. Programme refugees such as the Kosovans who came in 1999 were evenly dispersed throughout the country, but this occurred only because the programme was organised centrally by the Refugee Agency and the Department of Foreign Affairs. In contrast, when matters are left to the local authorities, as in the case of asylum-seekers, there is no dispersion. The imbalance is ludicrous. In late 1999, for example, Dublin was receiving over 1,000 asylum-seekers a week, while Co. Donegal was home to just two families. The council's expenditure on asylum-seekers for the year barely topped £2,000.

Clear evidence of the reluctance of many areas to accept their fair share emerges from correspondence between the Department of Health & Children and the Southern Health Board (SHB). The Minister for Justice, Mr O'Donoghue, wrote last year to the Minister for Health, Mr Brian Cowen, expressing his concern at the concentration of asylum-seekers in some parts of Dublin, 'particularly in the north inner-city area and Tallaght'. 'Meanwhile, there appears to be almost no such accommodation made available for them either on an emergency basis or in the private rented sector in Cork, our second largest urban area. This is unacceptable,' he wrote.[24]

In October 1999, the Department of Health & Children wrote asking the health board to source accommodation for asylum-seekers in its area. In a tart response the following month, the board pointed out that 50 per cent of the Kosovan refugees (i.e. not asylum-seekers) were being accommodated in its areas. Supplementary welfare, medical cards and health screening were the board's business; accommodation was not. 'The local authorities will provide fully for the accommodation requirements for asylum-seekers', the board responded, ignoring the fact that in Dublin, it is the EHB and not Dublin Corporation that has responsibility for these tasks. In addition, the SHB drew up a protocol on the provision of services to asylum-services, which describes the arrangements pertaining in the EHB area as 'unsatisfactory'.[25] Mr Cowen was forced to tell Mr O'Donoghue that the Southern Health Board had told him it was not the appropriate authority to provide accommodation for asylum-seekers. The EHB's position was followed with interest by the other health boards, and some were expected to adopt a similar stance.

The failure to disperse asylum-seekers throughout the state has been disastrous. Large numbers of immigrants have been dumped willy-nilly in the poorest parts of Dublin, leading to friction with local communities. Accommodation and support services have been stretched to the limit. The imbalance has created an inflated impression of the number of asylum-seekers and helped foster racism.

By October 1999, the EHB was turning away hundreds of accommodation-seekers from its office in the refugee applications centre every day. At least twelve Dublin hotels, some costing up to £100 a night, were pressed into service to provide emergency accommodation. When this option was exhausted, asylum-seekers were given money for rent and told to sort themselves out. Some managed to stay with friends or compatriots; others slept rough until the authorities were in a position to help them. One African woman and her three children spent the night in a city-centre park until UNHCR officials intervened and persuaded the EHB staff to find her a hotel room.

Amazingly, there is clear evidence that the authorities had been fully warned of this impending crisis at least eighteen months before it happened. Documents obtained under the Freedom of Information Act show that Dublin Corporation wrote to the Department of Justice in early 1998 regarding the shortage of accommodation and suggesting dispersion as a solution. The matter was discussed at an inter-departmental meeting of civil servants on 19 March, 1998, at which the EHB revealed that for the first time it had not been able to provide accommodation for all applicants. 'As it was likely that this would occur again in the near future, some asylum-seekers might have no option but to sleep rough', the EHB official told the meeting.[26] Yet it seems this prescient warning from an official who was bound to know the realities of the situation went unheeded. No action was taken and the accommodation time-bomb ticked away for another eighteen months before exploding late last year. Not until October 1999 was the matter taken in hand at the highest level. The government established a central directorate for asylum-seekers, acting under the auspices of the Department of Justice, in a belated effort to achieve some co-ordination. However, the sight of the department taking on the unlikely mantle of accommodation searcher and provider was ample proof that other areas of government were at best 'hastening slowly'.

The failure to process applications speedily had another unexpected effect. Many of those waiting in limbo for a decision from the authorities have put down roots here, forming friendships, relationships – and more. Hundreds of children have been born in Ireland to asylum-seeker parents over the past few years. These children are Irish citizens, and their parents therefore enjoy constitutionally defined rights to care and guardianship. The authorities used to grant residency to asylum-seeker parents of Irish-born children automatically, but when the numbers increased they ceased this practice. This was yet another clumsy and petty initiative, which did nothing to clear the backlog of cases or improve the image of the Department of Justice. Constitutionally, the department didn't have a leg to stand on. No judge would consent to the deportation by the state of the parent of an Irish-born child. Ironically, lawyers believe the protections were further strengthened by the constitutional changes brought forward in the Republic in 1999 as a result of the Northern Ireland peace agreements.

The department does have a problem, one that has been identified by the staff in Dublin's three maternity hospitals. It is clear that some women are exploiting the fact that anyone born in Ireland is automatically an Irish citizen, and have therefore travelled here specifically with the intention of giving birth in Ireland. Usually, their interest lies more in the consequent right of travel and residency elsewhere in the EU rather than in any specific entitlement to stay in Ireland. However, the department's 'shotgun' approach, by suspending the processing of residency applications for all asylum-seeker parents of Irish-born children, indiscriminately caused problems for all people in this category, and needlessly so. For a time, asylum-seekers were invited to withdraw their asylum applications, and instead to pursue a residency claim. Not surprisingly, most refused to do so. Eventually, in 1999, the authorities relented and started processing residency claims once again. The Department of Social, Community and Family Affairs estimated in August 1999 that between 500 and 800 people were seeking to remain in the state on the basis of being the parent of an Irish-born child.

The Media

The response of the Irish media to the arrival of large number of asylum-seekers in recent years has been characterised by inconsistencies, inaccuracies, exaggerations and generalisations. In their search to find stories to fill a quiet news-day, newspapers have on numerous occasions denigrated an entire category of vulnerable people. The sensitivity that usually applies in stories about Irish people has been lacking in many articles journalists have written about asylum-seekers. Emotive language has been widely used to whip up widespread fear of the new arrivals. Journalists have based many of their stories on the word of a single anonymous source, usually a Garda, without seeking any independent verification.

The language used has been slanted to suit the journalist's agenda; for example, Andy King has contrasted the 'deluge' language used by many journalists with the 'haemorrhage' and 'draining of lifeblood' language used in relation to Irish emigration. Many of these failings are borne out by the following selection of newspaper headlines:

- 'Services face overload as refugee flood continues' – *Sunday Business Post*, 18/5/97
- 'Why Irish Eyes aren't smiling on the great Romanian invasion' – *Irish Independent*, 23/5/97
- 'Floodgates open as a new army of poor swamp the country' – *Sunday World*, 25/5/97
- 'Crackdown on 2,000 "sponger" refugees' – *Irish Independent*, 7/6/97
- 'Gardaí move on dole fraud by daytrip refugees' – *Irish Independent*, 5/5/97

At the height of the media hysteria, the *Evening Herald* reported that 'large numbers of work-shy people from Eastern Europe and beyond are trawling the Internet to see which European country had the best social welfare system and were targeting Ireland as a place to seek refugee status'. No evidence was offered for the assertion. The security correspondent of the *Irish Independent* wrote about a 'a public outcry over the numbers flooding the country' and said there was 'a danger that genuine refugees will be swamped by the illegals'. But what evidence was there for this 'public outcry'? A banner headline on the front page of the *Sunday Independent* on 9 August, 1998, proclaimed: 'Asylum-seekers fake torture – Nigerian plot to falsify torture and rape evidence for asylum'. Again, the story was based on anonymous sources and contained mostly vague detail of the alleged plot. In any case, the majority of the alleged criminals weren't even asylum-seekers. The headline defamed an entire nation, mimicking the worst anti-Irish excesses of the British press.

In other anti-refugee stories, women were warned to stay off the streets for fear of 'refugee rapists', while taxi-drivers told how they smuggled asylum-seekers like cattle across the Border. On the radio, phone-in programmes delivered a relentless diet of callers complaining about refugees in explicitly racist terms.

None of these articles or programmes mentioned the fact that Ireland was receiving proportionately fewer asylum-seekers than its European neighbours, that the 'floods' mentioned comprised only a few thousand individuals or that virtually no evidence of fraud or organised smuggling had been produced.

The most astounding example of anti-asylum-seeker reporting – and one that should be studied in journalism schools for years to come – appeared in *The Wexford People* of 29 July, 1998, following the arrival in Rosslare port of forty-seven Romanians in a freight container the previous week. An extraordinary front-page editorial and several articles mingled internal contradictions, incitement to hatred and the plain bizarre in spectacular fashion. The editor, Ger Walsh, claimed the 'latest influx' of asylum-seekers had brought public services in the town 'to breaking point', though a representative of the local health board in the accompanying article baldly denied this. Mr Walsh said there was evidence of growing racial tensions, but he offered none. The authorities had 'no difficulty' providing top-of-the-range accommodation for the Romanians at a time when cash could not be found to build houses, it was claimed. 'The situation has not been helped by incidents in which old ladies living alone have felt under threat and where potatoes and vegetables were dug up and stolen from a garden in John Street by a group of refugees.' The article continued: 'There is also the fear that some young male asylum-seekers are intent on striking up deep personal relationships with impressionable young local girls, fully aware that a baby would ensure a pass-port to permanent residence in this country.' He concluded:

> The annoyance of many ordinary Wexford people who are struggling to make ends meet is understandable when they see new arrivals dressed in the latest designer shirts and jeans, eating their meals in a down-town restaurant and relaxing on the balcony of their apartment in an exclusive block, with the bills for their entire way of life being picked up by the Irish taxpayer.

Even at the height of this media frenzy, Wexford never had more than 200 asylum-seekers living there. A year after the article appeared in the *Wexford People*, *The Irish Times* reported there were just ninety-three asylum-seekers in the town. The housing officer of the local county council said the situation 'was blown out of all proportion'.[27]

Almost all of the newspapers mentioned above are owned by the Independent group, and Andy Pollak of *The Irish Times* has argued convincingly that the reporting of the issue by these newspapers 'fuelled misinformed intolerance' of refugees:

> There were far too many sensational headlines, mis-leading statistics, unsourced claims, and often plain demonising of asylum-seekers. Refugees, a small,

frightened and powerless group in Irish society had no
comeback against the big guns of the country's most
powerful media combine.[28]

Not all newspapers have been so prejudiced in their coverage of
asylum-seekers, but there is an unmistakable shallowness to
much of the coverage, even when it is favourable to the new
arrivals. In summary, cute babies and young women are 'good';
wary young men are not.

At the end of its year-long onslaught against refugees and
asylum-seekers, the *Irish Independent* ran an opinion poll into
public attitudes on the issue.[29] The survey was a classic exercise
in self-fulfilling prophesies. To no-one's surprise, the newspaper
found that a large majority of Irish people had very negative attitudes towards refugees. Only 10 per cent felt that all or most
asylum-seekers were genuine in that they faced danger or persecution in their own countries. The story ran on page one under
the headline 'Most oppose "open door" policy on refugees'.

The Irish Times made its own foray into opinion polling on
the subject in January 2000, and the outcome was equally ques-
tionable. The paper found that a substantial majority wanted
'strict limits to be placed on the number of refugees allowed into
the State'.[30] 'Despite the overwhelming support for strictly
limiting the number of refugees entering the State, a majority of
the electorate also favours taking a more generous approach to
refugees and immigrants,' the page-one story related. The
newspaper found the results 'apparently contradictory' and
claimed, in an editorial, that public opinion was 'sharply diver-
gent'. The Minister for Justice, Mr O'Donoghue, may be closer to
the public mood on immigration than previously thought by
many, including the PD Minister of State, Ms O'Donnell, the
reporter mused.

Perhaps Mr O'Donoghue is in tune with the public mood. The
point, though, is that no such deduction could be made from this
appallingly flawed exercise in cage-rattling. For a start, look at
the question posed in the survey. People were asked if 'we

should take a more generous approach than at present to refugees and immigrants in view of our own history of emigration and our current prosperity?' They were also asked whether 'the number of refugees allowed into the country should be strictly limited?' But as letter-writers to *The Irish Times* were quick to point out, these questions are so riddled with hidden assumptions and misleading descriptions as to be useless. Are there differences between 'refugees' and 'immigrants'? If so, should they not be considered separately? The reference to 'our own history of emigration' is an irrelevancy, though obviously placed there to tweak the conscience of the respondent and encourage the kind of result a liberal newspaper would like to see. No wonder the outcome was contradictory.

Even worse, though, the poll refers to 'refugees' – no mention of asylum-seekers – and seems to suggest some sort of quota could be applied to refugee numbers for the convenience of Ireland alone. The questions show an appalling lack of knowledge of human rights law. Either people qualify as refugees under the 1951 Convention, or they don't – Western states don't have a 'pick-and-choose' option. Would Ireland be satisfied to send back opposition leaders from Afghanistan into the hands of the Taliban, or Chechyen leaders to Russia, simply because a self-defined quota had been filled? It was disappointing, if not surprising, that even the most balanced newspaper should commit these errors three years after the issue first came to prominence. The media in general have failed to internalise or properly analyse the issues involved, and the result is a treatment of refugees and asylum-seekers that veers between the bumbling and the vicious. Much of the media coverage has appalled rank-and-file journalists, and the National Union of Journalists has made spirited efforts to encourage its members to write more balanced copy. The tide of anti-refugee stories ebbed somewhat in 1999, and the tabloids moved on to other topics – for now.

We like our refugees packaged, pretty and temporary. Contrast the above articles with the wildly enthusiastic articles written about the thousand or so Kosovan refugees who came to Ireland in the summer of 1999. 'Miresevini!' [Welcome] screamed the *Evening Herald* on its front page when the first group of Kosovans arrived at Farranfore airport in Co. Kerry. 'Rain-kissed and sincere – it was a typical Kerry welcome' the paper enthused. 'Refugees Swap Hell for Irish Heaven', declared the *Irish Sun*, over a picture of a smiling John O'Donoghue with an eight-year-old refugee on his knee. When it comes to a photo-opportunity, refugees – even those whose anonymity is supposed to be protected by law – are grist to the politican's mill.

Journalists have written their refugee stories safe in the knowledge that these nameless, wordless, powerless people are in no position to seek redress. The law of libel is the only rule that modern-day journalists absolutely wish to adhere to, and it simply doesn't apply in the case of subjects who have no money and no access to wealthy lawyers.

The legal system and the courts

As in so many other areas of Irish life, the defence of the rights of ordinary people – in this case, asylum-seekers and refugees – and the assertion of principles of international human rights have been left to the courts. The High Court's decision in the Fakih case made the 1985 letter from the Department of Justice to the UNHCR legally binding. In 1999, the High Court declared part of the 1935 Aliens Act unconstitutional, sending the Department into a spin and prompting the introduction of emergency legislation within weeks. Ironically, then, that the problem of providing legal aid for asylum applicants has proved so difficult to resolve. The Irish Refugee Council, a well-meaning but chronically under-funded body, terminated its legal advice service in September 1997 due to lack of resources.

In May 1998, the department sought tenders for the establishment of an 'independent' refugee legal service. But although a number of applications were received, the tender was abandoned and no contract was awarded. On the urging of the department, the Legal Aid Board subsequently agreed to provide the service. At present, the department pays £120 towards the legal costs of an appeal, though the actual cost is at least £360. Legal aid is available only at the appeal stage, so applicants are expected to fend for themselves in the initial stages of dealing with an unfamiliar Irish legal system, often in a language that is foreign to them.

It took one of the government's own refugee appeals commissioner, Peter Finlay, to identify most clearly the defects in this system. In December 1999, he told *The Irish Times* that people had not had free and independent legal advice from the outset of the asylum procedure.[31] Most asylum-seekers complete their initial questionnaire without the benefit of the free legal advice which is available from the Refugee Legal Service, he pointed out. Few attend for interview at the Department of Justice with a solicitor or legal advisor in attendance. Many of the interviewers are retired Gardai and, according to Finlay, the interviews consequently 'have all the hallmarks of a Garda interview in a station. But the one ingredient is missing: these people are not being accused or charged with any offence'. Finlay also expressed alarm at some of the decisions taken by the Department after the first-stage interview, which in his view would not bear up to public scrutiny. 'The legal standards applied to them are lower than would be applied to Irish people and their fundamental rights are not observed during the asylum process,' he said. After hearing 400 cases in eighteen months, Finlay came to the view that he was presiding over 'a travesty of a system,' one that 'bears all the hallmarks of a narrow and prejudiced state of mind'.

The department counter-attacked through its usual mouthpieces in the media, such as the security correspondent of the *Irish Independent*. Not surprisingly, Finlay and the Department parted company shortly afterwards, and the commissioner resigned in January 2000.

And what of the politicians, the Minister for Justice aside? In the early 1990s, the Fine Gael TD Alan Shatter introduced the first modern asylum bill into the Dail. This never became law but greatly influenced the Refugee Bill drawn up subsequently. Labour assigned a minister of state, Joan Burton, to the task of seeing the bill through the Oireachtas. This took longer than expected, mainly due to the number of amendments tabled, many of them minor. The result was that Labour left office shortly after the bill became law. The new Fianna Fail/Progressive Democrat coalition inherited legislation that was not of their making, and not to their liking.

The demise of the Refugee Act and the course subsequently embarked upon by the Minister for Justice and his department has been charted in these chapters. But if the minister could be accused of a knee-jerk response to the asylum issue, so too could the opposition. Far too often the opposition parties confined themselves to formulaic criticisms of government policy and easy jibes directed at Minister O'Donoghue; seldom did they inspire any confidence in their understanding of or empathy with asylum-seekers.

It took one of Mr O'Donoghue's colleagues, PD junior minister Liz O'Donnell, to make the most pungent and intellectually coherent assessment of her own government's record. In November 1999, Ms O'Donnell described policy on asylum-seekers as 'doom-laden and *ad hoc*' and called for an end to the 'administrative shambles':

> What is going on is a disgrace. The issue must be addressed through good, joined-up governance. It requires specific co-ordinated action by positively focused civil servants and ministers. To date this has not happened.[32]

Even this short extract from her remarks to the *Sunday Business Post* contains everything that was lacking in government statements up to then: the admission of failure up to now; the rejection of theories that Ireland was about to be 'flooded' or 'invaded' by asylum-seekers; an acknowledgement of the lack of coordination between departments; and a call for positive thinking.

The remarks sparked a mini-crisis in government, and a flurry of denials from Fianna Fáil ministers. Yet they seemed to make an impact, and new proposals were announced shortly afterwards on updating asylum and immigration law, and on issuing additional work permits to non-nationals.

A complete lack of understanding and compassion marks out the treatment of asylum-seekers in the Ireland of the 1990s. Voluntary groups have tried to help – for example, with accommodation, education and legal representation – where the state was often unwilling to meet its responsibilities fully. The price of official incompetence has been enormous in terms of exchequer expenditure and the waste of human potential. However, the real price of official neglect and demonisation has been paid by asylum-seekers both as a group and individually, as the next chapter demonstrates.

5. A refugee's lot – the wetbacks of Europe

The depressing realisation struck me that I was now really a homeless man, a fugitive, and under police surveillance . . . We set out for Strasbourg without further delay. However, the actual goal of my journey was Switzerland. (The prefect in Strasbourg) informed us that the French government had decided to intern the refugees. There was no way he could give us passports to enter Switzerland . . . so we secretly decided to proceed there even without official authorisation.[33]

Even those who are well disposed towards refugees can sometimes lose themselves in the statistics or legal issues involved. It's easy to forget that people's welfare and even their lives are at stake. Events of the past few years have had a profound effect not only on asylum-seekers but on all members of ethnic minorities living in Ireland. Whether they are Irish citizens or not, non-white residents have borne the brunt of a heightened sensitivity about race and colour. Racial abuse has become almost commonplace, and the veneer that allowed Irish people believe they lived in a tolerant society has been stripped away. In October 1997, the Department of Justice decided that all asylum-seekers would be issued with a new identity card. Several thousand people were required to turn up at its offices in Dublin. On a wet and windy Saturday afternoon, the queue stretched all along one entire side of St Stephen's Green. Men, women and children were left to stand for hours in the rain. Asked to comment on the matter, a spokesman said the department 'could not be blamed for the weather'.

For the department, it was an administrative mess and a public-relations disaster. But observers of government policy were less surprised. The fiasco merely demonstrated what was already apparent: that the asylum policies of the government and the department completely lacked a human dimension.

A world in motion

The scale of human migration is greater than ever before. Better and cheaper air travel, the creation of the 'global village' and the spread of television have all made the world's population better aware of life in other regions – and of the ways to get there. 'Push' factors such as war, famine and economic disintegration are more pervasive than ever. Ninety per cent of refugees still move from one Third World country to another, but the number making the greater leap to the West is increasing all the time. According to the International Centre for Migration Policy Development in Vienna, between 150,000 and 300,000 people successfully entered western Europe in 1998 without visas, joining anywhere from two to five million people already living illegally on the continent. In 1997 alone, German guards detained more than 35,000 'illegals'.

Little attention is paid in the asylum debate to the conditions that force people to flee. The issue is wrapped up in assumptions about Western levels of prosperity and human rights, when these simply do not apply in vast areas of the world. About half the world's population lives in poverty – that's 3 billion people – and 1 billion live in extreme poverty, defined by the UN as living on less than $2 a day. Over seventy countries are racked by war, executions and human rights abuses, according to reports from organisations such as Amnesty International and Human Rights Watch. In the Democratic Republic of Congo, for example, war and other upheavals have forced almost 1 million people to flee their homes. Of these, 272 came here last year.

In Sudan, the civil war has killed 1.9 million people and made over 4 million homeless. Some thirty-eight Sudanese came to Ireland in 1999. Nineteen asylum-seekers came from Burundi in 1999; Tanzania took in over 30,000 fleeing Burundians in November alone. Even Nigeria, which is not generally perceived as a country of crisis, has seen considerable violence. Over fifty people were killed in Lagos in November, 1999, during ethnic clashes. In the South of the country, more than 2,000 Odi people were reportedly killed by government soldiers.[34] Almost 2,000 Nigerians claimed asylum in Ireland in 1999.

The number of illegal migrant workers in the world is increasing by more than 6 million a year, earning organised crime an estimated $7 billion a year.[35] The International Labour Organisation estimates there are now more than 30 million illegal immigrants worldwide, most of them in developing countries. Human trafficking is estimated to be as large as the illegal drugs trade, with charges anywhere from $500 to $3,000.

Most refugees leave their homes with nothing, because they have nothing to lose. But some pay an even higher price for their desperation. The number of asylum-seekers who lose their lives during the flight from home is increasing all the time. In May 1997, for example, three Romanian asylum-seekers who had stowed away on a container ship were left to drown off the coast of Canada after being forced off a Taiwanese ship into the sea. The ship's crew said they were given no life-jackets, just bits of Styrofoam tied to their waists. The asylum-seekers didn't have proper papers and the shipping company could have been fined $6,000 per person if the captain had landed them. One group of Romanians who came to Ireland in summer 1998 spent four days and nights cooped up in an airless, windowless freight container. Carrying only the clothes they wore and small bags with food and water, they used plastic bags as toilets. A woman from Sierra Leone told Gardaí in Cork in April 1999 that the body of her two-year-old son who died on board a cargo ship en route to Ireland was dumped overboard by smugglers whom she had paid to get her out of Africa.

For many, their struggle has not ended with arrival in the rich West. Asylum-seekers have also died in their sometimes frantic efforts to stay in western Europe and avoid being sent back to their home countries. In May 1999, for example, a thirty-year-old Sudanese asylum-seeker, Amir Ageeb, died after a struggle with German police who were escorting him on to a Lufthansa flight for Cairo. The resultant outcry forced the authorities to suspend deportations temporarily. In September 1999, a twenty-year-old Nigerian woman, Semira Adamu, died in Belgium after policemen who were trying to deport her pressed her face into an airplane seat cushion to stifle her screams. She lost consciousness, and fell into a coma; the two policemen faced criminal charges, and the Belgian minister of the interior resigned over the ensuing scandal.

Racism and racist violence

After the desperate struggle to escape their homelands, it might be hoped that refugees would enjoy peace in their new-found sanctuaries in the West. But this has not happened, no less in Ireland than anywhere else. The generosity of Irish people to Third World charities was often put forward as evidence that they were not or could not be racist; however, some writers now say this phenomenon proves the opposite. Charity-giving, especially the 'Black Baby' syndrome of earlier decades, was posited on a sense of superiority on the part of the giver. It was also understood that the recipient was situated a great distance away. However, when the object of such pity is competing in the same socio-economic system for scarce resources, the reaction may be different. One non-governmental organisation leader quoted by Gertel[36] likened humanitarian feelings towards refugees to concerns about animal welfare: 'One wouldn't want to be competing with a dog for a job, nor would you invite a dog to the dinner table. Offering pity and compassion are evidently not the same as offering human dignity and equal opportunity.'

Surveys on the level of racism in Ireland have produced mixed results. Fr Micheal MacGreil's landmark book, *Prejudice and Tolerance in Ireland*, found that 'a relatively severe degree of racial prejudice' existed in Dublin in 1977. But when he revisited the subject several decades later, Fr MacGreil noted a significant *decline* in racism. This he attributed to positive role models such as the rock singer Phil Lynnott and the soccer player Paul McGrath and the strength of the anti-apartheid movement in Ireland. However, Fr MacGreil noted that the Irish brand of racism was 'largely vicarious and dormant'. His research was carried out before the arrival in Ireland of large numbers of asylum-seekers, many of them non-white.

A 1985 survey found that in Ireland 24 per cent of those interviewed considered that people of different race or culture should live in different districts. Twelve per cent admitted they were racially prejudiced. In 1989, 93 per cent of people said they were happy to have an English person living next door to them, but this figure fell to 63 per cent in the case of 'blacks'.[37] Regardless of what the surveys tell us, it is abundantly clear that the environment for all non-whites – whether Irish or not – has deteriorated markedly in the past few years. The selective, scare-mongering response of some media and the authorities to the increase in asylum-seekers stoked the flames of racism in wider society, resulting in an outpouring of racist abuse directed at anyone considered to be a refugee.

A 1998 survey of international students at Irish universities reported a relatively low level of discrimination on campus, but found relatively high levels of racial discrimination in wider society. More than 60 per cent of the students surveyed had experienced discrimination and this figure rose to almost 90 per cent in the case of non-white students. Verbal abuse, staring, stereotyping and physical assault were the most common incidents reported.

A high level of institutional racism was also recorded. As the authorities tightened immigration controls in 1997, many of the students bore the brunt of the new checks. A number of them detailed how all 'European-looking' people were allowed to pass rapidly through immigration while all apparently non-white passengers were stopped by the officials. In July of that year, CIE employees reported that Garda Special Branch detectives, acting as immigration officers, were boarding the Dublin-Belfast trains and asking rail staff if there were 'any black people' on board. Several non-white people have written to this author over the past few years to relate their experience of being singled out at immigration controls. In one letter, the (white) Irish mother of a black teenager told of her daughter's distress at being marked out as 'different' after she was singled out for questioning while passing through immigration in Dublin Airport. 'She sobbed herself to sleep, saying repeatedly "why didn't they stop any other Irish person",' her mother wrote in 1997.

The Association of Refugees and Asylum-seekers in Ireland has documented dozens of unprovoked attacks on immigrants in recent years. Few of these have been confirmed as racist attacks by the Gardaí, which considers most as examples of more straightforward violent assault. However, the racist element in some of the attacks is undeniable, and Gardaí in some inner-city areas of Dublin were at one stage advising asylum-seekers not to go out at night. Landu Kulubatulu, a seventeen-year-old Congolese youth, was racially abused before being slashed with a bottle in the worst single incident in 1998. He received seventeen stitches in the head. In the same year, a student from Sierra Leone remonstrated with three young men on the South Circular Road in Dublin who had shouted racial insults at him. His reward was to be badly beaten while passers-by ignored what was happening. A Zairean man had the same experience in broad daylight in Temple Bar in the city, and again passers-by failed to intervene. Mostly, though, non-white asylum-seekers and Irish people have to endure end-less taunts, insults and thoughtless remarks as they go about their daily lives.

Somewhere in the background, a few propagandists are circulating leaflets inciting hatred against blacks. One of these which has been in circulation intermittently over the past few years rails – in extremely bad English – against

> the worthless scum of the British Empire – traitors to their own countrys in Africa who cowardly joined the British enslaved, suckers who wanted to befriend them rather than fight them . . . They will outpopulate us and take over . . . they have bought up most of the houses and shops . . . Blacks breed lots of children for more dole.

Under the heading 'Keep Ireland Green and White' it goes on to claim bizarrely that 'blacks' keep 'snakes at home so they can drink their blood'.[38]

Politicians who speak out in favour of asylum-seekers frequently receive racist, abusive letters from anonymous correspondents opposed to immigration into Ireland. Teachers who encourage multi-racialism in their schools have also borne the brunt of such hate campaigns. Anti-immigrant sentiment has yet to find a coherent political voice in Ireland. While a number of backbench TDs and county councillors have expressed anti-asylum-seeker and often racist views, particularly during election campaigns, the mainstream political parties have shied away from any attempt to play the 'race' card to win votes. Fianna Fáil's Ivor Callely, a prominent critic of the new arrivals, can't mention the world 'asylum-seeker' without adding 'and illegal immigrants' in the same breath. In November 1999, his response to long queues at the Refugee Applications Centre in Dublin was to call for a 'get tough' policy towards asylum-seekers. He called on the government to 'throw out' illegal immigrants, claiming that many were cashing in on benefits.

However, while the political establishment hasn't shown moral leadership on the asylum-seeker issue, neither has it sunk to the depths seen in other Western European countries. In January 1998, the first avowedly anti-immigrant organisation came into being. The Immigration Control Platform was launched at a meeting in Ennis, Co Clare (Cullen, 1998).[39] The meeting was picketed by two groups of protesters, one of which prevented it from going ahead. In spite of widespread publicity and the indefatigable efforts of its founder, the Cork school-teacher Aine Ní Chonaill, the ICF has failed to attract significant support.

The Roma, a special case

> *Because, with the sole exception of the Jews, it is the Roma who have above all others suffered constant persecution and discrimination. And this injustice continues today.*[40]

The largest single ethnic group to come to Ireland in recent years has been the Roma. Not all Roma are from Romania, and not all Romanian asylum-seekers are Roma, but there is considerable overlap between the two categories. Because of their distinctive dress (in the case of the women) and because some have resorted to begging, the Roma have achieved prominence and notoriety in some quarters. For racists, the term Roma has become synonymous with asylum-seekers. When people complain in generalised terms about 'asylum-seekers', they are frequently talking about Roma.

Media portrayal has tended to perpetuate the clichéed image of the gypsy as a thieving rascal with a large family and money stashed away under the mattress. For example, when large numbers of East European Roma came to Britain in 1997, they were greeted with headlines such as 'Gypsies Invade Dover Hoping for a Handout' and 'They Speak Little English But Know Exactly How to Play The System'.[41]

Irish people could be forgiven for knowing little about an ethnic group seldom seen in this country before. However, it is not possible to consider the special case of the Roma without some knowledge of their history and background. Numbering about 8 million, they are Europe's largest minority, a people with a 500-year history in Europe of continuing mistrust, rejection and exclusion. In 1496, for example, a German edict declared the Roma 'traitors to Christianity'. In 1504, Louis XII forbade them to enter France and until late last century the Roma lived as slaves in Romania. The Nazis killed an estimated 500,000 Roma.

In modern-day Germany, thousands of Roma who fled violence in their native Romania have been greeted with sporadic neo-Nazi violence. Austrian hostels housing Roma asylum-seekers have been fire-bombed. Czech laws deny several thousand Romas citizenship in that country, effectively making them stateless. The US Department of State, in its report on human rights practices in Romania in 1997, said: 'The Romani population, estimated at approximately 2 million persons, continues to be subject to societal discrimination, harassment, beatings and violence.'

The European Roma Rights Center, in a 1996 report entitled, 'Sudden Rage at Dawn: Violence against Roma in Romania', summarised the situation as follows:

> Romani communities throughout Romania are today the target of systematically conducted police raids and our investigations into this police activity revealed gross violations of human rights and fundamental freedoms. Police brutality seems to have replaced the previous episodes of community violence.
>
> Victims' and witnesses' statements lead to the conclusion that the pattern of abuse is the same: the police arrive in large numbers, heavily armed and in the company of dogs. They come early in the morning – at dawn – and do not present warrants or explain the reasons for their actions. They break into the homes of Roma, force them out of bed and bring them to the police stations for interrogation. In most cases, victims and witnesses reported severe ill-treatment by the police.[42]

Amnesty International remains concerned about the protection of fundamental human rights in Romania. In March 1998, it was continuing to receive reports of human rights violations, including the imprisonment of prisoners of conscience, torture and ill-treatment of detainees as well as police shootings in disputed circumstances. The organisation criticised the failure of authorities to investigate earlier human rights violations inflicted on Roma. As one sympathetic refugee landlord put it to me: 'No-one, nowhere, wants them, and isn't that what being a refugee is all about?'

6. What happens now? – options for the future

Ireland today stands at an important crossroads in its dealings with asylum-seekers and other immigrants. Many mistakes have been made in the past decade, but it is not too late to put many of these to rights. Once the historical backlog of over 6,000 cases has been dealt with, the slate will have been wiped clean again and a fresh start can be made.

This time, there can be no excuses, no special pleading of ignorance or lack of resources. This state is bound in more tightly than ever before to the global economy, and it cannot fail to take on the responsibilities that go with this position. It has dealt with the asylum-seekers of the 1990s, and learned from that experience. With its new economic might comes a duty to do more to alleviate suffering in the world, and part of this entails taking a greater share of the refugee burden.

Every state, Ireland included, has a right to regulate the flow of people across its borders. It has the right to adjust this in accordance with economic, social and cultural priorities. Our small population, and the relative size of our neighbours, makes it imperative that migration is strictly monitored and controlled. New legislation and new controls will undoubtedly be necessary in the future to meet changing circumstances. However, legislation and immigration controls alone are an insufficient response to the asylum issue. To pursue such a policy risks repeating the failures of the past few years. The success of the Celtic Tiger has led to widespread labour shortages that can only be relieved through immigration. On both humanitarian and economic grounds, some of this should come from outside the EU. But creating a greater racial mix in Ireland should be seen as a desirable thing not just from an economic point of view; some of the most vibrant and successful communities in the world derive their strength from a heady mix of cultures and races.

Critics can point to some parts of the world where this mix has gone badly wrong. Ireland, however, is well placed to avoid these failures. Ghettos are usually the result of government inaction and policies that socially exclude minorities. Unfortunately, this is what has happened up to now. Asylum-seekers were prevented from working until the modest measure that allowed some of them to take up employment was introduced in July 1999 (see chapter 5). Access to education has also been barred in most cases. Most have been accommodated in the poorest parts of Dublin, in areas already suffering from unemployment, crime and social exclusion. Small wonder, then, that tensions have arisen between the established poor and the new arrivals.

'The policy of putting asylum-seekers into a limbo of several years' duration, where they are prohibited from working, and they and their families discouraged from learning English, is souring the whole induction process for immigrants', says Fr Bill Toner, director of the Jesuit Centre for Faith and Justice in Dublin.[43] There are clearly differing opinions on whether a multi-ethnic Ireland is a good thing or not. But this misses the point, which is that rapid change is inevitable over the coming years. Indeed, it has already begun, and the only thing that matters now is how to regulate this change. If it wasn't already happening because of the pressure of immigration, our EU partners would be demanding that Ireland take its fair share of asylum-seekers. Doing nothing in the 1990s has created a major social problem and cost the exchequer millions; battening down the hatches on immigration could end up damaging the economy. But being proactive and putting humanitarian considerations first would mean that Ireland as a prosperous Western state was finally playing its part in alleviating suffering in the world. Its pronouncements on international human rights could be taken more seriously and its standing with the Third World would increase.

The most important initial contribution the state could make now is to decouple the debates about asylum and immigration. For too long now, these two issues have been confused, often by those who preferred to muddy the waters deliberately. Economic migrants have used the asylum procedure to come to Ireland simply because there is no other means open to them. The situation is the same throughout Europe, where nearly every state has virtually eliminated immigration. The UNHCR has described this state of affairs as 'very unhealthy'. As explained in previous chapters, the definition of asylum is very tightly drawn, so that many of those who do not qualify as official asylum-seekers may nonetheless be deserving cases. However, in the heated terms in which the debate has been conducted here in recent years, all asylum-seekers have been stigmatised as 'bogus'. As a result, the status of asylum, a cornerstone of international human rights law, has become debased.

One way the government could act to reverse this trend would be to become more actively involved in sharing the burden of high-risk refugees with other Western states. We do this to some extent already in the case of programme refugees such as the Kosovans or Bosnians, but not for individual convention refugees. Unlike many other Western countries, Ireland has no standing resettlement quota for refugees who cannot find safety in their first country of asylum.

On every continent, there are people who are in extreme danger, or who have languished for years in a refugee camp, whose lives could be immeasurably improved if they were given sanctuary in the West. On immigration, the case for establishing an annual quota for people from outside the EU has won widespread support in all sections of society. Such a quota would be flexible, and closely tied in to the economic situation. It would give the authorities the opportunity to exercise more control over the kind of immigrants it wants than it has at present, and could prove invaluable in filling skills shortages. At the same time, it could also favour the most needy and deserving cases.

Toner has suggested a quota of about 4,000 a year, separate from those seeking asylum. He points out that the Economic and Social Research Institute has forecast that an additional 285,000 employees will be required between 1995 and 2003.[44] As the boom continues, even this forecast is beginning to look over-cautious.

There remains the issue of the thousands of asylum-seekers who came here in the 1990s and who are still awaiting decisions. More and more of these cases are nearing the end of the process, though for some this has lasted years. The proportion of successful applicants is less than 10 per cent at first instance, but the newly formed appeals authority is overturning up to one-third of rejections at appeal stage. The failure to arrive at the 'right' decision first time around is only costing more money. Many groups have called for an 'amnesty' for these applicants. This would allow the authorities to clear their books and free their attentions for new arrivals. But such a measure would be completely indiscriminate, and largely unfair in that it would reward those who have, effectively, pushed their way to the front of a very long queue. An amnesty would completely devalue the concept of asylum by granting refugee status to people regardless of the merit of their cases. All refugees would suffer as a result.

The best course for the government to follow in respect of these cases is to expedite all asylum applications, while ensuring that fair and thorough procedures are being followed. Those who have applied for asylum would at least be put out of the agony of waiting. There is a case for a 'fast-track' approach to applicants from severely disrupted countries, for example, Somalia, Algeria or Sierra Leone. In the past few years, the Irish authorities have refused applications from individual asylum-seekers from each of these countries basing their decisions on a narrow interpretation of the 1951 Convention. But no sensible government is going to send back an asylum-seeker from such war-torn states, for practical and humanitarian reasons. Even if the department were prepared to brazen out the inevitable public outcry, could it find an airfield safe enough to land a plane on in Mogadishu or Freetown? So why go through the charade and expense of application and appeal, when there is no possibility of deportation?

Under an expedited system, some asylum-seekers would be successful, either in the first instance or at the appeal stage. Those who are unsuccessful should not be automatically deported. Because of the extraordinary and inexcusable delay in handling their cases – many asylum-seekers have spent years in a bizarre administrative limbo which was no fault of their own – the government should have strong regard to the humanitarian dimensions of the issue. Many asylum-seekers have settled and put down roots in Ireland in the time they have been waiting for their cases to be heard. Circumstances have changed in their home countries, often for the worse. Where are they to go to? There is a strong case for allowing many of those who have waited for several years leave to stay here on humanitarian grounds. This should be a once-off gesture, as the authorities now recognise that they cannot afford to permit a recurrence of the backlog of the past few years.

Much more could be done to ease the situation of asylum-seekers in Ireland. There is a strong case for dispersing new arrivals throughout the country. This would distribute the burden more equitably, ease the pressure on the poorer parts of Dublin and prevent the formation of ghettos. The government's initial moves in this direction have been uninspiring. There is little point, and even less justice, in dispersing people to areas where they have no support structures, where no-one speaks their language, and where no allowance is made for their culture or eating preferences.

In April, 2000, the government intends to introduce direct provision, under which asylum-seekers will receive vouchers in place of the present cash payments. But the experience of other countries shows that such a system delivers fewer savings than governments hope. In Germany, for example, vouchers have been found to be cumbersome and unwieldy to administer.

Many shops refuse to accept vouchers and those that do frequently charge more. Georg Classen of the Berlin refugee organisation, Pro Asyl, has calculated that it costs his government £2,200 a month to keep a family with three children in a one-roomed flat in a Red Cross hostel, when it would cost only £920 if the family were aided directly.[45] 'The government is spending vast amounts of money on refugees, but it is businessmen, not the refugees themselves, who are profiting,' he says. But then maybe that's the attraction.

Asylum-seekers should be given freer access to education, and the teaching of English-language skills should not be left to voluntary groups. The Department of Education has begun to respond to the needs of refugee children and there is no reason why other government departments should not work harder to integrate adult asylum-seekers. The sad experience of Vietnamese asylum-seekers, many of whom have still not mastered English twenty-five years after coming to Ireland, should not be forgotten. Integration of refugees and long-term asylum-seekers poses a variety of challenges for the authorities. Apart from the issuing of work permits, there is the question of travel documents and the facilitation of visits by and to other members of the family.

It isn't just asylum-seekers who need education and assistance with integration; there is evidence that much more needs to be done to educate Irish people about other cultures and the challenges of living in a multi-ethnic society. The authorities need to take a more pro-active role in countering the negative images and stereotypes propagated by the media and, yes, government departments. So far, it seems that many people's experience of other cultures derives from restaurant-eating and nothing more sophisticated than that.

The Department of Justice will also have to address the thorny issue of citizenship. There is ample evidence that the provision in the Constitution that bestows Irish citizenship on all persons born here is being abused. Dublin maternity hospitals have reported a significant rise in the number of non-nationals having children in Ireland; many, it seems, have arrived solely for the birth. Because of this trend, the department stopped for a time issuing residency permits to parents of Irish-born children, a move that affected both genuine asylum-seekers who have had children since coming here and others intent on profiting from this legal loophole. However, altering the law in this area may first require an amendment to the Constitution.

Ultimately, when all stages of the process and the law have been exhausted, there will be considerable numbers of deportations from Ireland. Up to now, because of the delays and the lack of fair procedures, there have been good reasons for arguing against deporting asylum-seekers and other immigrants. Many of these have been explored in the courts, which have invariably found in favour of deportees. However, deportations are an essential element in the asylum system. They are necessary to safeguard the integrity of the process, a fact that has not been digested by all the groups supporting asylum-seekers. It can only be hoped that the immigration authorities will carry them out in a responsible and restrained manner.

As we enter into a new Millennium, a new form of enlightened self-interest is called for. Ireland, as one of the twenty richest democracies in the world, must finally take its place among the nations of the Western world who are committed to sharing the burden of suffering in other regions. We cannot partake so successfully in the global movement of goods and services without recognising that people, too, cross borders, and sometimes for good. We have to learn that there is more to multi-racial societies than ethnic restaurants, that pluralism can be a force for economic and social growth, and that the asylum-seekers of today are the spiritual heirs of generations of Irish emigrants over the past 150 years.

Glossary

Asylum
A place of refuge for people in need of protection for reasons of race, nationality, membership of a particular social group or political opinion.

Declaration of Human Rights, 1948
'Everyone has the right to seek and to enjoy in other countries asylum from protection'.

Asylum-seeker
A person seeking protection here and subsequent recognition as a refugee by the Department of Justice. An asylum-seeker is in effect making an application to *become* a refugee. More than 18,000 people applied for asylum in Ireland between 1992 and the end of 1999.

Ethnic group
An ethnic group is a group of people who share a common identity by virtue of their heritage, culture, history and tradition.

Humanitarian leave to remain
This status is afforded to individuals who do not meet all the official requirements for full refugee status, but do prove to be in a refugee-like situation or other individual considerations giving strong reason to allow them to stay. Status can be afforded on a temporary or review basis. Fewer than seventy people have been given leave to remain in Ireland since 1992.

Immigrant
Immigrants are people who choose to come to Ireland for reasons related to their standard of living or economic situation. They are not fleeing persecution. In order to immigrate to Ireland legally the individual must first seek permission from the state before arriving.

Illegal immigrant
An illegal immigrant is a person who comes to Ireland seeking

work or a better standard of living without permission from the state and without official documentation such as a work visa.

Non-refoulement
The principle whereby no person may be forcibly returned to a territory where his or her life or freedom may be threatened on account of his or her race, religion, nationality, membership of a particular social group or political opinion.

Refugee
This term is used in a global sense to describe an individual fleeing persecution. In the official domestic sense, the Department of Justice uses it to identify those people who have successfully achieved recognition as being in need of protection and resettlement and therefore have *become* refugees. About 1,000 people have been granted refugee status so far, two-thirds on appeal.

Programme refugees
comprise a group of people judged by the government as being in special need of protection. As in the case of the Vietnamese boat people in the 1970s, the Bosnians in the early 1990s and the Kosovans in 1999, they are granted refugee status, with the attendant benefits, as a group. Generally, they enjoy the same welfare and other rights as Irish nationals, and may apply for citizenship after three years of residency.

Convention refugees
have their cases judged individually, according to the criteria laid down in the 1951 Geneva Convention Relating to the Status of Refugees. The majority of asylum-seekers who have come to Ireland in recent years are seeking recognition as programme refugees. Those formally granted refugee status are entitled to take up employment and to receive health, education, social welfare and other benefits on the same basis as Irish nationals.

The 1951 definition of a refugee has entered Irish legislation as:

> a person who, owing to a well-founded fear of being
> persecuted for reasons of race, religion, nationality,

membership of a particular social group or political opinion, is outside the country of his or her nationality and is unable to, owing to such fear, is unwilling to avail himself or herself of the protection of that country; or who, not having a nationality and being outside the country of his or her former habitual residence, is unable or, owing to such fear, is unwilling to return to it.

Residency

If an asylum-seeker has a child born in Ireland, the child automatically becomes an Irish citizen. The child's parents then become eligible for residency status, which is renewable annually. Since 1992 more than 1,300 people have been granted residency.

Notes

1   Ward, TCD, 1996.

2   Gertel, 1999, p. 2.

3   National Archives, the Department of the Taoiseach, file S11007, 25 October, 1946, cited in Gertel, p. 22.

4   See Ward, Eilis, 'Ireland and Refugees/Asylum-seekers 1922–66', paper presented to conference 'The Expanding Nation: Towards a Multi-Ethnic Ireland', ed. Ronit Lentin, Trinity College Dublin, September 1998. It appears the Hungarians expected Ireland to be an intermediate, rather than a final, place of refuge.

5   Ward, Eilis, 'A big show-off to show what we could do' – Ireland and the Hungarian Refugee Crises of 1956. Irish Studies in International Affairs, Vol. 7, page 140.

6   Gertel, 1999, p. 4.

7   Gertel, 1999, p. 1.

8   Refugees, United Nations High Commissioner for Refugees, Geneva, Switzerland, vol. II, no 113, 1998, p. 6.

9   Austrian politics lurched to the right in February 2000 after the conservative People's Party agreed to form a coalition with the far-right Freedom Party led by Dr Jorg Haider. The Freedom Party is avowedly anti-immigrant.

10 Cited in Refugees, p. 12.

11 Department of Justice figures, 1998.

12 Official figures.

13 Byrne, R., page 108 (see bibliography).

14 'Wanted: An Immigration Policy' in Working Notes, issue 33, Jesuit Centre for Faith and Justice, December 1998, p. 8.

15 Bernard McDonagh, second secretary at the Department of Justice, Equality and Law Reform, speaking at the Oireachtas Committee on Social, Community and Family Affairs, reported in The Irish Times, 23 September, 1998.

16 Michael Begley in 'Asylum in Ireland: A Public Health Perspective', 1999, cited in The Irish Times, 30 November, 1998.

17 Faughnan, 1998, p. 12

18 Ward, 1998.

19 In the case of Ahmed Hussein Fakih, Ali Hamdan and Mohammed Anis Slim v The Minister for Justice (Irish Reports, 1993), the High Court held that this letter was binding on the Minister for Justice.

20   Interdepartmental Committee on Non-Irish Nationals (1994) Interim Report on Applications for Refugee Status. Dublin: Stationery Office.

21   Working Notes team, Toner, p. 12

22   Faughnan, 1998, p. 9.

23   Mr O'Donoghue also announced plans to outlaw trafficking in illegal immigrants in June 1999. The bill proposes large fines and terms of up to ten years in prison.

24   Quoted in *The Sunday Tribune*, 2 January, 2000

25   Quoted in *The Sunday Tribune*, 2 January, 2000

26   *The Irish Times*, 22 February, 2000.

27   *The Irish Times*, 19 May, 1999.

28   Pollak, p. 45.

29   Pollak, p. 42.

30   *The Irish Times*, 24 January, 2000.

31   *The Irish Times*, 4 December, 1999.

32   *The Sunday Business Post*, 14 November, 1999.

33   *Refugees*, United Nations High Commissioner for Refugees, Geneva, Switzerland, vol. II, no. 113, 1998, p. 5.

34   *The Irish Times*, 13 January, 2000.

35   Report from International Confederation of Free Trade Unions, Brussels, 1998.

36   Gertel, p. 12.

37   The Committee of Enquiries into the Rise of Fascism and Racism in Europe, cited in Gertel, p. 10.

38   Anonymous circular sent to author, 1997.

39   Report on meeting in the following day's edition of *The Irish Times*, 14 January, 1998.

40   Guenther Grass, Index on Censorship, 4/98, July 1998.

41   First newspaper headline, *The Independent,* 20/10/1997.

42   European Roma Rights Center, *Sudden Rage at Dawn: Violence against Roma in Romania*, Budapest, September 1996.

43   Working Notes, p. 6.

44   Economic and Social Research Institute of Ireland, *Occupational Employment Forecasts 2003*, November 1997.

45   Interview with author, September 1999.

Bibliography

Boucher, G. *The Irish are Friendly, but . . .: A Report on Racism and International Students in Ireland*, Irish Council for International Students (ICOS), Dublin, November 1998.

Byrne, R., 'On the Sliding Scales of Justice: the Status of Asylum-seekers and Refugees in Ireland' in *Developments in Discrimination Law in Ireland and Europe*, R. Byrne and W. Duncan (eds), Irish Centre for European Law, Trinity College, Dublin, 1997, pp. 107–17.

Commission on Emigration and other Population Problems, report, Government Publications, Dublin, 1956.

Cullen, P., chapter on 'Ireland' in *Extremism in Europe: 1998 Survey, European Centre for Research and Action on Racism and Anti-semitism*, CERA, Paris, 1999.

European Roma Rights Center, *Sudden Rage at Dawn: Violence against Roma in Romania*, Budapest, September 1996.

Faughnan P., 'A Healthy Voluntary Sector – Rhetoric or Reality?' in *Reflections on Health*, J. Robins, (ed.), Department of Health, Dublin 1997, pp. 232–49.

Gertel, Shulamith, 'The Insular Society: Irish Society and Immigration – An Historical Point of View', *Sociological Papers* Vol. 7, No. 1, Sociological Institute for Community Studies, Bar-Ilan University, Israel, January 1999.

King, Andy, *Porous Nations: From Ireland's Haemorrhage to Immigrant Inundation*, Paper presented at Conference 'The Expanding Nation: Towards a Multi-Ethnic Ireland', Trinity College, Dublin, September 1998.

MacGreil, Micheal, *Prejudice in Ireland Revisited*, Survey and Research Unit, St Patrick's College, Maynooth 1996.

McVeigh, Robbie, *The Racialisation of Irishness: Racism and Anti-Racism in Ireland*, Centre for Research and Documentation, Belfast, 1996.

National Union of Journalists, *Racism in Ireland: The Media in Focus*, conference report, February, 1998.

O'Regan, C., *Report of a Survey of the Vietnamese and Bosnian Refugee Communities in Ireland*, Refugee Resettlement Research Project, Refugee Agency, June 1998.

O'Sullivan, Eoin, *Homelessness, Housing Need and Asylum Seekers in Ireland*, A report for the Homeless Initiative, Dublin, 1997.

Pollak, Andy, 'An Invitation to Racism? Irish Daily Newspaper Coverage of the Refugee Issue' in *Media in Ireland: The Search for Ethical Journalism*, Open Air, Dublin, 1999.

Toner Bill, 'Wanted: An Immigration Policy', *Working Notes*, Issue 33, Jesuit Centre for Faith and Justice, Dublin, December 1988.

Trocaire/The Irish Commission for Justice and Peace, *Refugees and Asylum-seekers: A Challenge to Solidarity*, researched and written by Jerome Connolly, ICJP, and Maura Leen, Trocaire, Dublin, December 1997.

Ward, E., 'Ireland and Refugees and Asylum-seekers: A Critical Overview of State Policy', paper presented to conference, 'The Expanding Nation: Towards a Multi-Ethnic Ireland', Trinity College, Dublin, September 1998.